Food and Nutrition

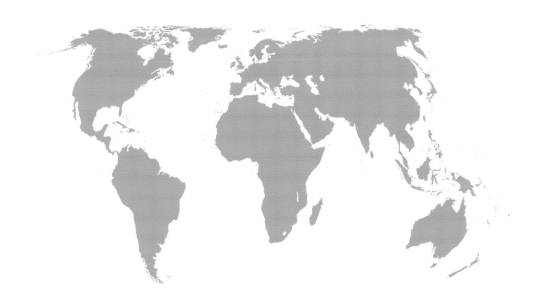

WORLD ALMANAC® LIBRARY

Contents

Food and Nutrition

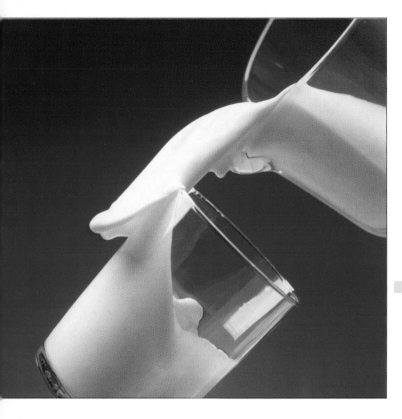

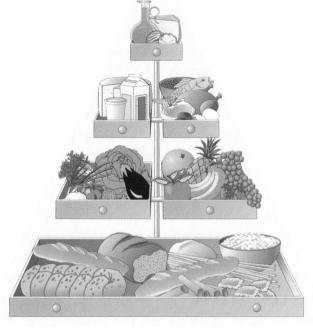

Please visit our web site at: www.worldalmanaclibrary.com
For a free color catalog describing World Almanac® Library's list of high-quality books and multimedia programs, call 1-800-848-2928 (USA) or 1-800-387-3178 (Canada). World Almanac® Library's fax: (414) 332-3567.

Library of Congress Cataloging-in-Publication Data available upon request from publisher. Fax (414) 336-0157 for the attention of the Publishing Records Department.

ISBN 0-8368-5617-1

This North American edition first published in 2004 by
World Almanac® Library
330 West Olive Street, Suite 100
Milwaukee, WI 53212 USA

This U.S. edition copyright © 2004 by World Almanac® Library.
Original title: *Alimentazione—Vivere e sopravvivere.* Italian Edition:
© GEOnext—ISTITUTO GEOGRAFICO DE AGOSTINI S.p.A., Novara, 2002
Developed by the editorial and cartographic staffs of
GEOnext - Istituto Geografico De Agostini S.p.A. - Novara

Translation by: N.C.M Servizi srl
World Almanac® Library editor: Jim Mezzanotte
World Almanac® Library cover design: Scott M. Krall

Maps of Our World
4 Planet Earth
6 World Climates
8 Europe: Agriculture and Fishing
10 Asia: Agriculture and Fishing
12 Africa and Oceania: Agriculture and Fishing
14 The Americas: Agriculture and Fishing

Undernourishment
(% variation over the total
number of undernourished people)

Improving
situation

Worsening
situation

Peru
Chad
Ghana
Kuwait
Mozambique
Malawi
Angola
Sudan
Togo
Thailand
Vietnam
China
Iraq
Guatemala
Mongolia
Somalia
Venezuela
Cuba
Tanzania
Burundi
North Korea
Dem. Rep. of the Congo

-30   -20   -10   0   10   20   30

What We Eat and Drink
16 Food as a Necessity: Vital Fuel
18 Plants and Animals: Links in the Food Chain
20 Nutrients
22 Water: An Indispensable Resource

Food and Civilizations
24 Origins of Agriculture: Domestication of
    Plants and Animals
26 The Spread of Agriculture
28 Wheat and Rice
30 Other Important Crops
32 Beverages

Agriculture and Fishing
34 Agriculture Today: Different Methods
36 Livestock and Fish
38 Producing More Food: Innovative Methods
    and Techniques
40 The Green Revolution

The Economy of Food Resources
42 Large Food Producers
44 World Food Trade

46 Agribusiness
48 Economic Problems: Dependence
    of Developing Countries
50 Science and Agriculture

Food and Populations
52 Food Availability: A Delicate Balance
54 The Magnitude of Hunger
56 Disasters and Resources
58 Healthy Eating Habits
60 Nutrition and Society: The Role of Women
62 Food as Culture: Languages, Religions, Taboos

64 **Food Availability Statistics**

70 **Glossary**

79 **Index**

Planet Earth

ALB. ALBANIA (Tiranë)
A. ANDORRA (Andorra la Vella)
ARM. ARMENIA (Yerevan)
AUS. AUSTRIA (Vienna)
AZER. AZERBAIJAN (Baku)
BEL. BELGIUM (Brussels)
B.H. BOSNIA AND HERZEGOVINA (Sarajevo)

BULG. BULGARIA (Sofia)
CR. CROATIA (Zagreb)
EST. ESTONIA (Tallinn)
G. GEORGIA (T'bilisi)
HUNG. HUNGARY (Budapest)
ISR. ISRAEL (Jerusalem)
LAT. LATVIA (Riga)

LEB. LEBANON (Beirut)
L. LIECHTENSTEIN (Vaduz)
LIT. LITHUANIA (Vilnius)
LUX. LUXEMBOURG (Luxembourg)
MAC. MACEDONIA (Skopje)
MOLD. MOLDOVA (Chişinău)
M. MONACO

NETH. NETHERLANDS (Amsterdam)
R. RUSSIA
S.M. SAN MARINO
S.-M. SERBIA AND MONTENEGRO (Belgrade)
SLOV. SLOVAKIA (Bratislava)
SL. SLOVENIA (Ljubljana)
SWITZ. SWITZERLAND (Bern)

World Climates

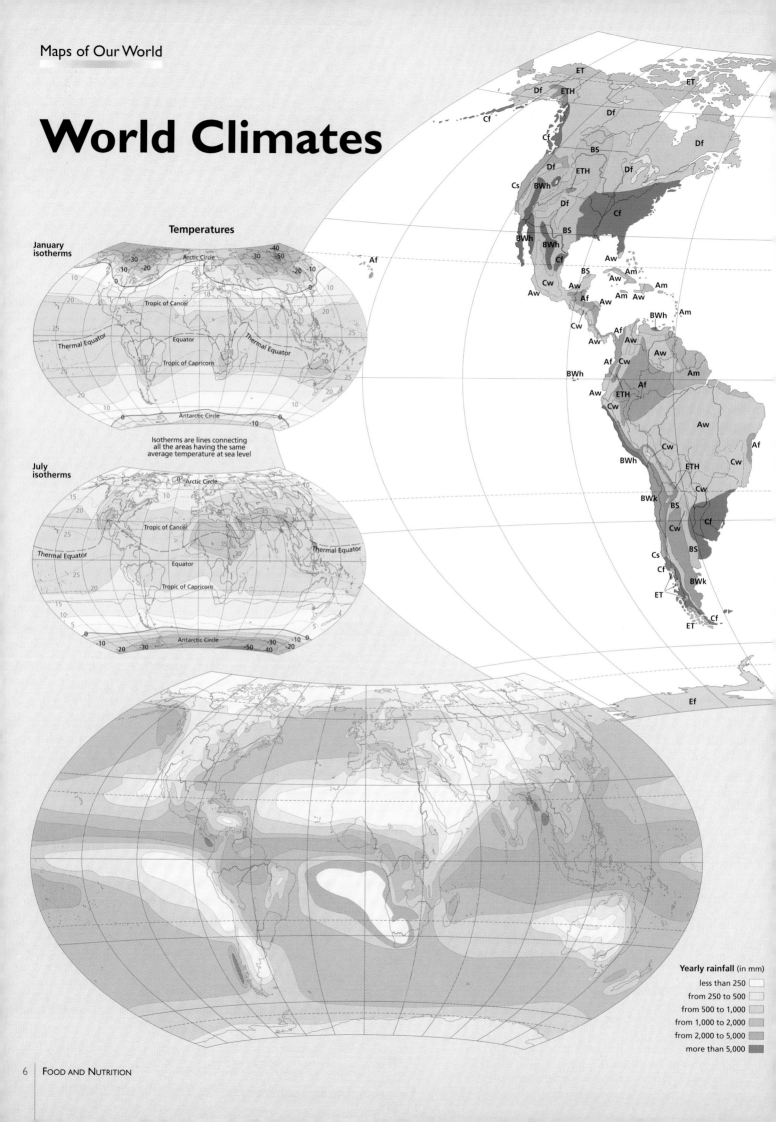

Temperatures

January isotherms

July isotherms

Isotherms are lines connecting all the areas having the same average temperature at sea level

Yearly rainfall (in mm)

- less than 250
- from 250 to 500
- from 500 to 1,000
- from 1,000 to 2,000
- from 2,000 to 5,000
- more than 5,000

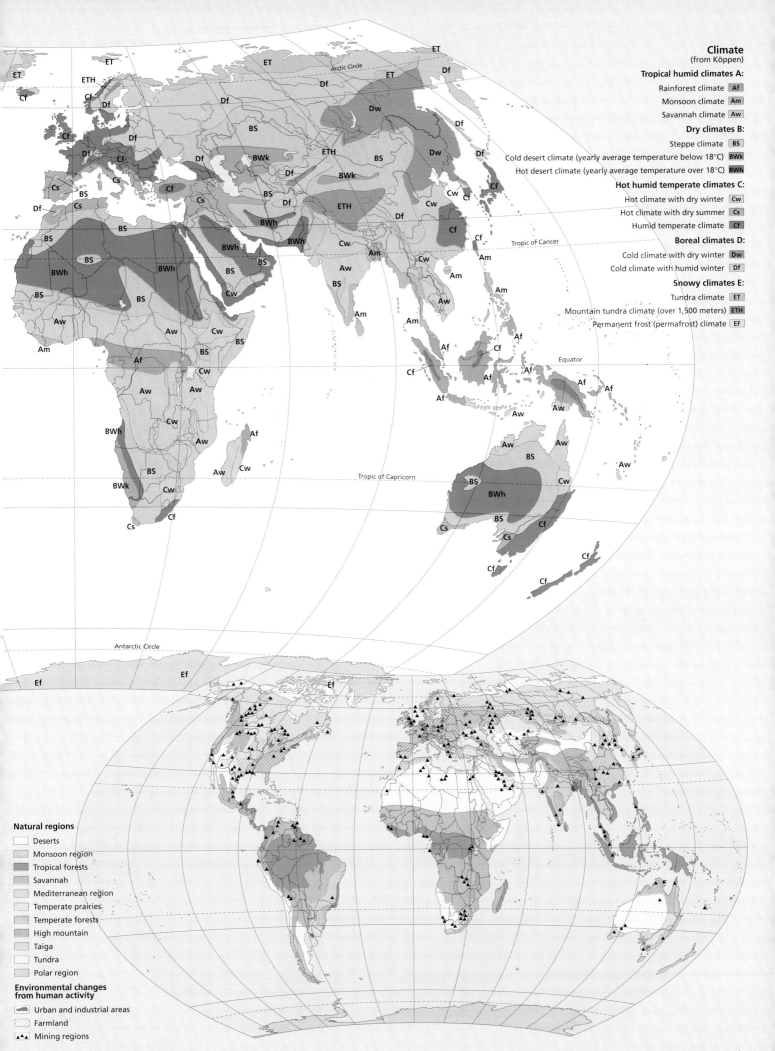

Tropical humid climates A:

Rainforest climate `Af`

Monsoon climate `Am`

Savannah climate `Aw`

Dry climates B:

Steppe climate `BS`

Cold desert climate (yearly average temperature below 18°C) `BWk`

Hot desert climate (yearly average temperature over 18°C) `BWh`

Hot humid temperate climates C:

Hot climate with dry winter `Cw`

Hot climate with dry summer `Cs`

Humid temperate climate `Cf`

Boreal climates D:

Cold climate with dry winter `Dw`

Cold climate with humid winter `Df`

Snowy climates E:

Tundra climate `ET`

Mountain tundra climate (over 1,500 meters) `ETH`

Permanent frost (permafrost) climate `EF`

Arctic Circle

Tropic of Cancer

Equator

Tropic of Capricorn

Antarctic Circle

Natural regions

- Deserts
- Monsoon region
- Tropical forests
- Savannah
- Mediterranean region
- Temperate prairies
- Temperate forests
- High mountain
- Taiga
- Tundra
- Polar region

Environmental changes from human activity

- Urban and industrial areas
- Farmland
- Mining regions

Europe
Agriculture and Fishing

Cod

Siglufjördur

Reykjavik

Cod

Akureyri

Seydisfjördur

Herring

Norwegian

Sea

Tromsø

Narvik

Cod

Bodø

Herring

Salm

Kristiansund

Ålesund

Trondheim

Herring

Herring

Bergen

Cod

Stavanger

Tønsberg

Oslo

Vänern

Stockolm

Shetland
Islands

North

Sandefjord

Skagen

Skagen

Vättern

Inveraray

Aberdeen

Hirtshals

Göteborg

Glasgow

Edinburgh-Leith

Thyborøn

Grenå

Kalmar

Herrir

Lie

Herring

Sea

Esbjerg

Baltic

Fleetwood

Kingston
upon Hull

Copenaghen

Klaipé

Dublin

Herring

Cuxhaven

Sassnitz

Puck

Manchester

Grimsby

Harlingen

Bremer-
haven

Rostock

Gdynia

Milford
Haven

London

Herring

Amsterdam

Hamburg

Wolin

Kalini

Mackerel

Ostend

Rotterdam

Elbe

Berlin

Vistule

Boulogne-
sur-Mer

Brussels

Rhine

Oder

Wars

ATLANTIC

Concarneau

Saint-
Malo

Fécamp

Dieppe

Douarnenez

Paris

Prague

Guilvinec

Lorient

Loire

Danube

OCEAN

Les Sables-
d'Olonne

Lyon

Munich

Vienna

Budape

La Rochelle

Tuna

Sardines

Bordeaux

Mackerel

La Coruña

Ferrol

Gijón

Oysters

Arcachon

Rhône

Turin

Milan

Chioggia

Zagreb

Vigo

Bermeo

St-Jean-
de-Luz

Marseille

Livorno

Ancona

Zara

Sardines

Belgr

Matosinhos

Pasajes

Vis

Figueira da Foz

Makarska

Lisbon

Madrid

S. Benedetto
del Tronto

Tagus

Mataró

Setúbal

Barcelona

Rome

Bari

Olhão

Huelva

Palma
de Mallorca

Crustaceans

Tuna

Naples

Cádiz

Algeciras

Málaga

Tuna

Tuna

Marsala

Mediterrane

Mazara
del Vallo

Tun

Soil use

Rocky, icy, sterile, barren areas
Tundra
Boreal conifer forest
Mixed temperate forest, woods
Meadows and pasture lands
Farmland
Steppe and shrubby prairies
Desert or semi-desert
Swampy areas or areas subject to floods
Irrigated areas
Intensive animal husbandry (dairy industry)
Grapevine northern limit
Wheat northern limit
Olive tree northern limit
Cork areas

Fishing

Large-scale fishing areas
Minor fishing areas
Large fishing ports

Crops

Wheat
Corn
Rice
Sugar beets
Citrus fruits
Grapevines
Olive trees
Potatoes

Barents Sea
Cod
Herring
mmerfest Vardø
Murmansk
Kandalakša
Salmon
Belomorsk
Archangel
Severnaya Dvina
Mezen'
Nar'jan Mar
Pecora
Lake Onega
Kuopio
ulu
Raahe
Lake Ladoga
Kama
ku Helsinki
inn St. Petersburg
iiumaa Pärnu
remaa
pils
Riga
Minsk
Volga
Moscow
Oka
Samara
Samara
Don
Volga
Kiev
Dnieper
Dnipropetrovs'k
Volgograd
Volga
Atyrau
Dniester
Taganrog
Don
Mariupol'
Rostov-na-Donu
Astrahan'
Sturgeon
Sturgeon
Odessa
Kerch
Mackerel
Novorossiysk
Bucharest
Danube
Caspian Sea
Mahačkala
Sofia
Burgas
Black Sea
Istanbul
Athens
Sponges
n S e a

Asia
Agriculture and Fishing

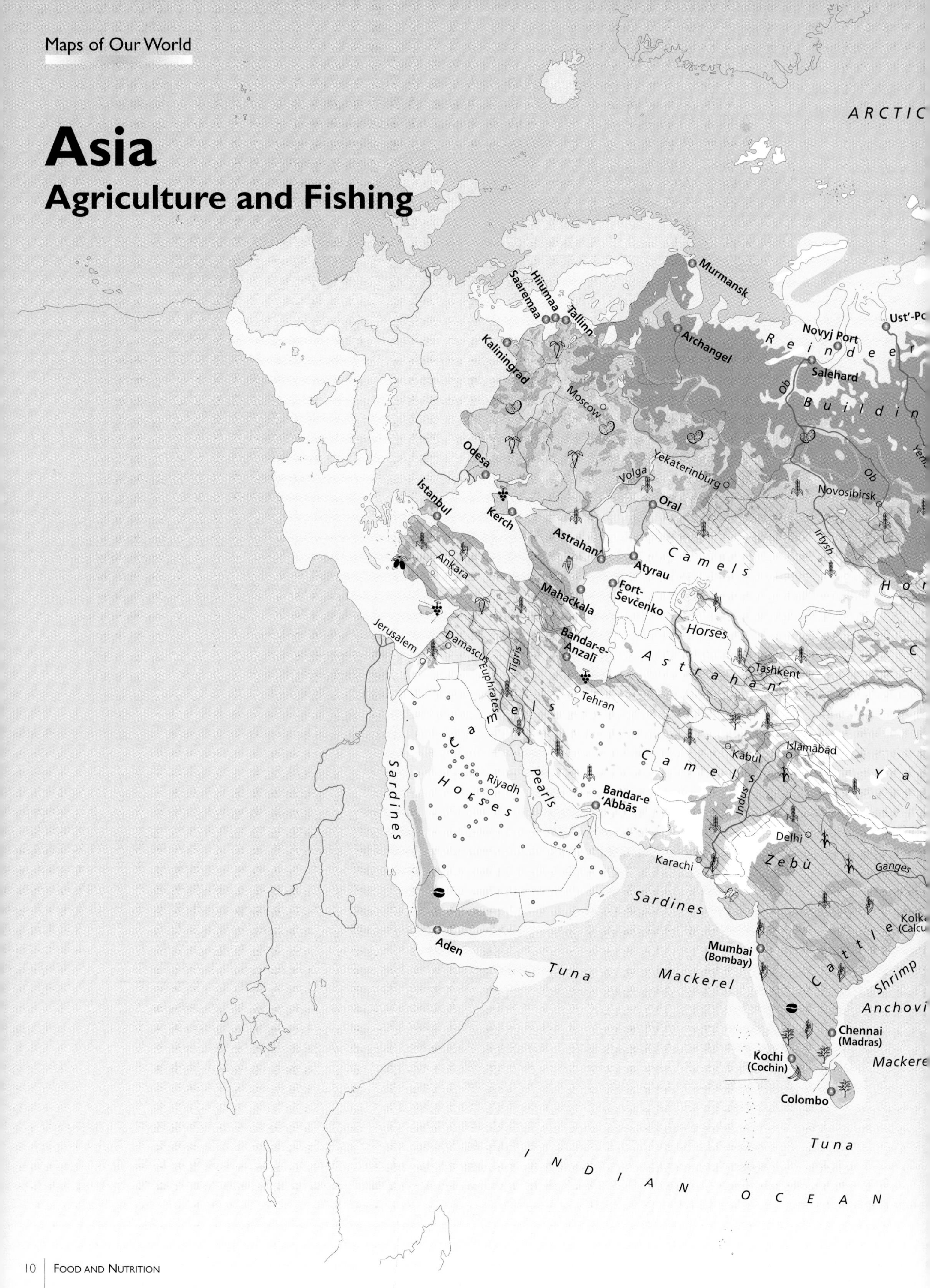

ARCTIC

Murmansk

Hiiumaa
Saaremaa
Tallinn

Novyj Port

Ust'-Po

Archangel

Kaliningrad

R e i n d e e

Salehard

Moscow

B u i l d i n

Ob

Odesa

Yekaterinburg

Novosibirsk

İstanbul

Volga

Oral

Yeni

Kerch

Astrahan

C a m e l s

İrtyš

Ankara

Astrahan

Atyrau

Ho

Mahačkala

Fort-
Sevčenko

Horses

Tashkent

Bandar-e-
Anzali

Jerusalem

Damascus

Euphrates

Tehran

A s t r a h a n'

Tigris

Kabul

Islamābād

Y a

C a m e l s

Riyadh

Pearls

Delhi

Zebù

Ganges

Horses

Bandar-e
'Abbās

Karachi

Indus

Kolk
(Calcu

Sardines

S a r d i n e s

C a t t l e

Shrimp

Mumbai
(Bombay)

Aden

Tuna

Mackerel

Anchovi

Chennai
(Madras)

Kochi
(Cochin)

Mackere

Colombo

Tuna

I N D I A N   O C E A N

Soil use

Rocky, icy, sterile barren areas
Tundra
Northern conifer forests
Temperate belt forests
Tropical rainforests
Steppe
Savannah
Desert or semi-desert
Oases ○
Farmland
Meadows and pasture lands
Animal husbandry
Wheat northern limit

Fishing

Large-scale fishing areas
Minor fishing areas
Large fishing ports ◉

Crops

Wheat
Corn
Rice
Sugar cane
Sugar beets
Apples
Bananas
Grapevines
Coffee
Tea
Soybeans
Peanuts
Olive trees
Oil palms
Coconuts
Potatoes

OCEAN

Seals
Seals
Seals
Reindeer
Salmon
Salmon
Whales
Cod
Tuna

Lena
Magadan
Ohotsk
Ust'-Bolšereck
Kihčik

Timber
Fur
Lena
Amur

Irkutsk
Camels
Ulaanbaatar

els

Abashiri
Nemuro
Rumoi
Kushiro
Otaru
Hachinohe
Nahodka
Hakodate
Shiogama
Aomori
Kimch'aek
Chōshi
Anchovies
Niigata
Tuna
Wŏnsan
Misaki
Namp'o
Inch'ŏn
Hamada
Shimizu
Beijing
Dalian
Pusan
Sardines
Tientsin
Yantai
Kōchi
Crustaceans
Tsingtao
Mokp'o
Aburats
Huang He
Nagasaki
Makurazaki

PACIFIC
OCEAN

Shanghai
Nanjing
Ningbo
Mackerel
Chang Jiang
Pigs
Fuzhou
asa
Canton
Xiamen
Macao
Hong Kong
Kaohsiung

Hanoi
Oysters
Haiphong
Anchovies
Manila

Teak
Rosewood
Mekong

Yangon
(Rangoon)
Bangkok
Ho Chi Minh City
Pearls

Pearls
Mackerel
Sea Cucumbers
Sea Cucumbers

Singapore

Ebony
Ujung Pandang
Turtles

Teak
Jakarta
Surabaya

Africa and Oceania
Agriculture and Fishing

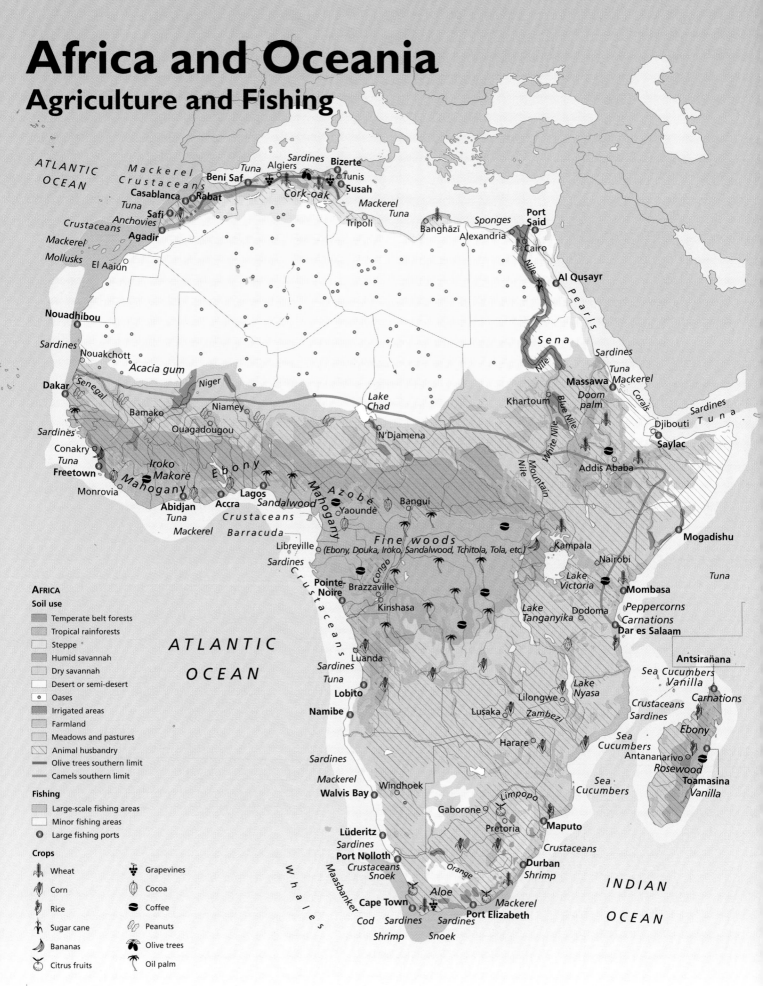

ATLANTIC OCEAN

Mackerel
Crustaceans
Tuna
Sardines
Algiers
Bizerte
Beni Saf
Tunis
Susah
Casablanca **Rabat**
Cork-oak
Tuna
Safi
Anchovies
Agadir
Crustaceans
Mackerel
Mollusks
El Aaiún
Mackerel
Tuna
Tripoli
Banghāzī
Sponges
Alexandria
Port Said
Cairo
Al Quṣayr

Pearls

Sena

Nouadhibou

Sardines
Nouakchott
Acacia gum
Niger
Khartoum
Sardines
Massawa
Tuna
Mackerel
Doom
palm
Corals

Dakar
Senegal
Bamako
Niamey
Lake Chad
White Nile
Blue Nile
Sardines
Tuna
Djibouti
Saylac

Sardines
Ouagadougou
N'Djamena
Mountain Nile
Addis Ababa

Conakry
Tuna
Freetown
Monrovia
Iroko
Makoré
Mahogany
Ebony
Mahogany
Azobé
Sandalwood
Lagos **Accra**
Abidjan
Tuna
Crustaceans
Mackerel
Barracuda
Yaoundé
Bangui
Kampala
Nairobi
Mogadishu
Tuna

Libreville
Fine woods
(Ebony, Douka, Iroko, Sandalwood, Tchitola, Tola, etc.)
Lake Victoria
Mombasa

Sardines
Crustaceans
Pointe-Noire
Brazzaville
Congo
Kinshasa
Lake Tanganyika
Dodoma
Peppercorns
Carnations
Dar es Salaam

ATLANTIC OCEAN

Sardines
Tuna
Luanda
Lake Nyasa
Antsirañana
Sea Cucumbers
Vanilla

Lobito
Lilongwe
Crustaceans
Sardines
Carnations

Namibe
Lusaka
Zambezi
Sea Cucumbers
Ebony

Harare
Antananarivo
Rosewood

Sardines
Sea Cucumbers
Toamasina
Vanilla

Mackerel
Windhoek
Limpopo
Walvis Bay
Gaborone
Pretoria
Maputo
Crustaceans
Shrimp

Lüderitz
Sardines
Port Nolloth
Crustaceans
Snoek
Orange
Durban

Whales
Maasbanker
Cape Town
Aloe
Mackerel
Port Elizabeth
Cod
Sardines
Sardines
Snoek
Shrimp

INDIAN OCEAN

AFRICA
Soil use
- Temperate belt forests
- Tropical rainforests
- Steppe
- Humid savannah
- Dry savannah
- Desert or semi-desert
- Oases
- Irrigated areas
- Farmland
- Meadows and pastures
- Animal husbandry
- Olive trees southern limit
- Camels southern limit

Fishing
- Large-scale fishing areas
- Minor fishing areas
- Large fishing ports

Crops
- Wheat
- Corn
- Rice
- Sugar cane
- Bananas
- Citrus fruits
- Grapevines
- Cocoa
- Coffee
- Peanuts
- Olive trees
- Oil palm

Garapan

Agana

Koror

Dalap-Uliga-
Darrit

P A C I F I C

Palikir

Bairiki

Vaiaku

Tuna

Madang

Sea Cucumbers

Port
Moresby

Crustaceans

Honiara

Vila

Suva

Sea Cucumbers

Darwin

Sea Cucumbers

*Artesian
basins*

Townsville

Noumća

Tuna

O C E A N

*Artesian
basins*

Carnarvon

Artesian basins

Lake
Eyre

Brisbane

Tuna

Mackay

Perth

Kalgoorlie-
Boulder

Darling

Sydney

Tuna

Port Lincoln

Adelaide

Murray

Canberra

Auckland

Tauranga

Whales

Crustaceans

*Artesian
basins*

Bega

Crustaceans

Crustaceans

Melbourne

Whales

Tuna

Crustaceans

Wellington

Christchurch

Timaru

Sole

Dunedin

Oceania

Soil use

☐	Rocky, icy, sterile, barren areas	
▨	Temperate belt forests	
▨	Tropical rainforests	
▨	Tropical dry forests	
☐	Shrubby and bushy steppe	
☐	Dry savannah	
▨	Humid savannah	
☐	Desert or semi-desert	
▨	Irrigated areas	

▨	Cultivated areas
▨	Meadows and pasture lands
▨	Animal husbandry
⋯	Intensive animal husbandry (dairy industry)

Fishing

▨	Large-scale fishing areas
☐	Minor fishing areas
⊙	Large fishing ports

Crops

🌾	Wheat	🍎	Apples
🌽	Corn	🍌	Bananas
🌾	Rice	🍇	Grapevines
🎋	Sugar cane	🥥	Coconuts

The Americas
Agriculture and Fishing

Crops

Wheat
Corn
Sugar cane
Sugar beets
Apples
Bananas
Citrus fruits
Grapevines
Cocoa
Coffee
Soybeans
Peanuts

ARCTIC OCEAN

Seals
Whales
Seals
Whales
Herring
Cod
Salmon

Salmon
Reindeer
Yukon Fort Yukon
Fur
Mackenzie
Great Bear Lake
Trout
Great Slave Lake
Seals
Sturgeon Trout
Churchill
Fur
Red fir, Jackpine
St. John's
Cod

Herring
Halibut
Ketchikan
Crustaceans
Prince Rupert
Salmon
Herring
Vancouver
Douglas fir, Red fir, Pine trees
Red fir, Tamarack
Edmonton
Trout
Lake Winnipeg
Regina
Winnipeg
Lake Superior
Lake Huron
Oak, Pine trees
Montreal St. Lawrence
Ottawa
Salmon
Trout
Lake Ontario
Canadian fir Maple Herring
St. John
Lobster
Mackerel
Halifax
Portland
Cod
Boston
Shrimp
New Bedford
Mackerel

Salmon
Crustaceans
Oysters Sharks
Columbia
San Francisco
Sequoia
Monterey
Sardines
Los Angeles
San Pedro
San Diego
Ensenada
Anchovies
Guaymas
Tuna
Sardines
Mackerel
Anchovies
Tuna

Red fir
Red fir, Pine trees
Denver
Missouri
Lake Michigan
Chicago
Lake Erie
Beech, Black walnut
Red fir
New York City
Baltimore
Washington, D.C.
Oysters
Crustaceans
Mackerel
ATLANTIC OCEAN

Arizona Pine
Colorado
St. Louis
Ohio
Oak, Black walnut
Mississippi
Atlanta
Shrimp
Pitchpine

Rio Grande
Dallas
Port Arthur
New Orleans
Twaite shad
Shrimp
Tuna
Twaite shad
Shrimp
Sponges
Pearls
Turtles

PACIFIC OCEAN

Pearls
Building Timber and Fine Woods
Tuna
Mexico City
Ciudad del Carmen
Havana
Manzanillo
Lake Nicaragua
Tuna
Crustaceans

NORTH AMERICA

Soil use

- [ ] Rocky, icy, sterile, barren areas
- [ ] Tundra
- [ ] Northern conifer forests
- [ ] Temperate belt forests
- [ ] Tropical rainforests
- [ ] Steppe
- [ ] Savannah
- [ ] Desert or semi-desert
- [ ] Swampy areas
- [ ] Irrigated areas
- [ ] Farmland
- [ ] Meadows and pasture lands

- Animal husbandry
- Intensive animal husbandry (dairy industry)
- Wheat northern limit

Fishing

- [ ] Large-scale fishing areas
- [ ] Minor fishing areas
- [ ] Newfoundland (cod fishing)
- Large fishing ports

ATLANTIC

OCEAN

Crops

Wheat

Corn

Rice

Sugar cane

Apples

Bananas

Citrus fruits

Grapevines

Cocoa

Coffee

Tea

Soybeans

Curaçao

Pearls

Santa Marta

Caracas

Carúpano

Maracaibo

Crustaceans

Georgetown

Whales

Cattle

Magdalena

Meta

Orinoco

Quassia

Bogotá

Guaviare

Crustaceans

Branco

Mackerel

Quito

Putumayo

Japurá

Rio

Negro

Manaus

Belém

Crustaceans

Guayaquil

Balsa

Amazon

Fortaleza

Anchovies

Marañón

Rosewood and Citron trees

Paita

Juruá

Brazil nut

Tuna

Ucayali

Purus

Madeira

Xingu

Tapajós

Tocantins

Araguaia

Carnauba

Parnaíba

Maceió

Sardines

Chimbote

Sheep

Huacho

Crustaceans

Guaporé

Salvador

Callao

Lima

Beni

Mamoré

Brasília

São Francisco

Swordfish

Lake

Titicaca

La Paz

Anchovies

Cattle

Ilo

Arica

Paraguay

Paraná

São Paulo

Crustaceans

Whales

Mackerel

Iquique

Pilcomayo

Asunción

Pigs

Rio de Janeiro

Santos

Herring

PACIFIC

OCEAN

Antofagasta

Quebracho

Tuna

Florianópolis

Salado

Uruguay

Paraná

Cattle

Valparaíso

Rio Salado

Buenos Aires

Rio Grande

Steppe

Santiago

Montevideo

Crustaceans

Cod

Concepción

Colorado

Anchovies

Mar del Plata

Chaco

Bahía Blanca

Tuna

Ancud

Sheep

Comodoro

Rivadavia

Cod

ATLANTIC

OCEAN

Río Gallegos

Crustaceans

Seals

Whales

Whales

Turtles

Whales

SOUTH AMERICA

Soil use

Rocky, icy, sterile, barren areas

Tundra

Temperate belt forests

Tropical rainforests

Dry forests

Steppe

Savannah

Desert or semi-desert

Swampy areas

Salty swamps

Irrigated areas

Farmland

Meadows and pasture lands

Animal husbandry

Wheat southern limit

Llama area

Fishing

Large-scale fishing areas

Minor fishing areas

Large fishing ports

Food as a Necessity
Vital Fuel

In order to survive, the human body needs a variety of substances, which are found in food. After the body has digested food, these substances supply it with energy and help it perform various tasks.

The main categories of substances needed by the body are proteins, carbohydrates, and fats. Proteins, which can be found in both plants and animals, are used by the body for building and repairing tissues and for carrying out different processes. Carbohydrates, which are found in foods such as cereals, fruits, and vegetables, are the body's main source of energy. Fats, which can come from both plants and animals, provide energy in a more concentrated form and help the body absorb certain vitamins. In addition, a balanced diet must provide other substances, such as vitamins and minerals, that have very specialized functions in the body.

Food energy value is measured in calories. The number of calories a diet must provide to an adult individual in twenty-four hours varies depending on a person's lifestyle, gender, and age, and ranges from 1,600 calories for a young woman to 3,500 calories for an adult male engaged in heavy work.

The criteria for evaluating food, however, is only partly related to nutritional value. There are other important aspects to be considered, such as taste, consistency, shape, level of intestinal absorption, digestibility, and the lack of any toxicity. In addition, there are different food habits to be considered. Depending on the availability of food, which is related to factors such as natural environment, climate, and history, different food habits have developed, and these habits have contributed to the characteristics of the world's many cultures.

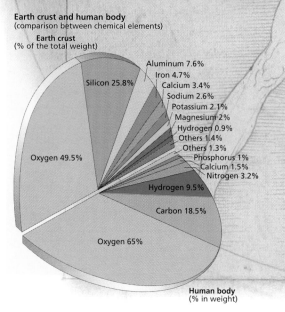

Earth crust and human body
(comparison between chemical elements)

Earth crust
(% of the total weight)

- Silicon 25.8%
- Aluminum 7.6%
- Iron 4.7%
- Calcium 3.4%
- Sodium 2.6%
- Potassium 2.1%
- Magnesium 2%
- Hydrogen 0.9%
- Others 1.4%
- Oxygen 49.5%

Human body
(% in weight)

- Others 1.3%
- Phosphorus 1%
- Calcium 1.5%
- Nitrogen 3.2%
- Hydrogen 9.5%
- Carbon 18.5%
- Oxygen 65%

Human body make-up

- Carbohydrates 1%
- Minerals 4%
- Fats 17%
- Proteins 19%
- Water 59%

(scale: 0, 10, 20, 30, 40, 50, 60, 70, 80, 90, 100)

CHANGES IN LIFESTYLES, CHANGES IN DIET

HUNTER-GATHERER PEOPLES

A project carried out by the European Food Information Council (EUFIC) has examined changes in the energy sources used by human beings, based on the development of the human race from prehistoric times to the modern era.

When humans were still hunter-gatherers, they relied on the protein and fat in the animals they killed, fish they caught, and bird eggs they collected. Starch (a kind of carbohydrate), fibers, and vitamins were found in the sprouts, berries, tubers, and edible leaves and flowers that were gathered, and salt consumption was almost nonexistent.

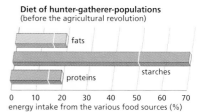

Diet of hunter-gatherer-populations
(before the agricultural revolution)

fats
starches
proteins

0 10 20 30 40 50 60 70
energy intake from the various food sources (%)

FARMING PEOPLES

Once people began raising crops and livestock instead of hunting and gathering their food, their diets changed drastically. Cereals became the most widespread plants grown, since they grew quickly and yielded large harvests. They were rich in starches, and, therefore, sugars. Honey became a precious source of sugar, while plants such as olive trees provided fats. Salt and fiber consumption increased considerably.

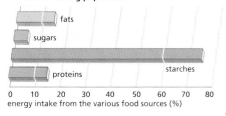

Diet of farming populations

fats
sugars
proteins
starches

0 10 20 30 40 50 60 70 80
energy intake from the various food sources (%)

PEOPLES IN INDUSTRIAL SOCIETIES

Food habits changed radically during the industrial revolution of the 19th century, when scientific discoveries led to advances in agriculture and food processing. At the beginning of the 19th century, for example, the first sugar beet processing factory was established in France, and sugar became available. Scientific discoveries also led to advances in wine and dairy production. The consumption of starch and fiber decreased, as people began to replace vegetables in their diets with foods that were richer in fats and salt.

Diet in industrial societies

fats
sugars
starches
proteins

0 10 20 30 40
energy intake from the various food sources (%)

Variations in diet in the United Kingdom from 1770 to 1970
(grams per person per day-estimate)

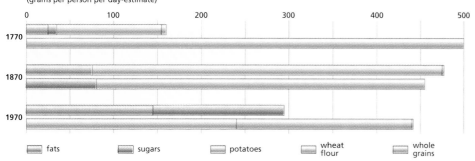

0 100 200 300 400 500

1770
1870
1970

fats   sugars   potatoes   wheat flour   whole grains

The chart at left shows the evolution of food consumption in the United Kingdom from 1770 to 1970. Note the constant decrease in the consumption of flours and cereal fibers and the huge increase in the consumption of sugars and fats. Many people like foods with a lot of fats. In addition to tasting good, these kinds of foods make a person feel full, since they stay in the stomach longer than other types of food.

Plants and Animals
Links in the Food Chain

A human being who lives to be at least 65 years old will usually eat more than 70,000 meals, which amounts to over 55 tons (50 metric tons) of food and an enormous amount of fluids. Humans are omnivores, which means they eat both plants and animals.

As omnivores, humans are at the top end of the food chain. At the other end of the chain are green plants, called producers. Through photosynthesis, they process organic substances from minerals contained in soil, water, and air. Higher up the food chain are the primary consumers—herbivores, or plant eaters. Higher still are are the secondary consumers—insectivores (insect eaters), carnivores (meat eaters), and omnivores—which mostly feed on organic substances (proteins, fats, carbohydrates, vitamins), taken from the animal and vegetable kingdoms. The chain is completed by decomposers, which turn dead organisms and organic waste into substances that can be used by plants. As omnivores, humans have always treated food with curiosity and caution—curiosity is needed to find new food

sources, but caution is needed because any new food could be dangerous. Earth has over 30,000 plant species that are considered edible, but only 7,000 of these species have become part of the food cycle, and only 3 account for 50 percent of the human diet.

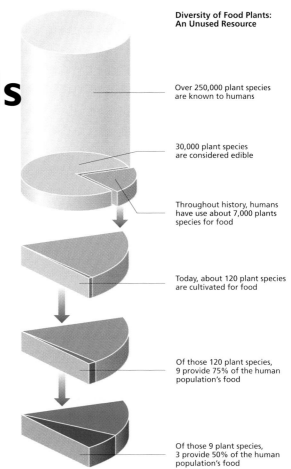

**Diversity of Food Plants:
An Unused Resource**

Over 250,000 plant species are known to humans

30,000 plant species are considered edible

Throughout history, humans have use about 7,000 plants species for food

Today, about 120 plant species are cultivated for food

Of those 120 plant species, 9 provide 75% of the human population's food

Of those 9 plant species, 3 provide 50% of the human population's food

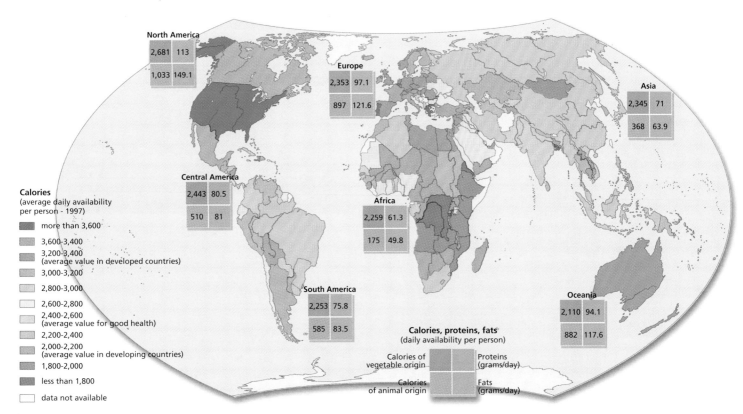

North America
2,681 | 113
1,033 | 149.1

Europe
2,353 | 97.1
897 | 121.6

Asia
2,345 | 71
368 | 63.9

Central America
2,443 | 80.5
510 | 81

Africa
2,259 | 61.3
175 | 49.8

South America
2,253 | 75.8
585 | 83.5

Oceania
2,110 | 94.1
882 | 117.6

Calories
(average daily availability per person - 1997)

- more than 3,600
- 3,600-3,400
- 3,200-3,400 (average value in developed countries)
- 3,000-3,200
- 2,800-3,000
- 2,600-2,800
- 2,400-2,600 (average value for good health)
- 2,200-2,400
- 2,000-2,200 (average value in developing countries)
- 1,800-2,000
- less than 1,800
- data not available

Calories, proteins, fats
(daily availability per person)

| Calories of vegetable origin | Proteins (grams/day) |
| Calories of animal origin | Fats (grams/day) |

Quinoa

Our diets must include food that can meet our daily need for various nutrients. Quinoa ("keen-wa") is a food that contains a balanced proportion of all nutrients. This plant has been grown as a crop in Latin America, particularly in the Andes region, for thousands of years. Called the "mother corn" or "corn of the gods," it is a cereal with a high percentage of protein and is also a good source of fibers, complex carbohydrates, fats, minerals, and vitamins.

Quinoa was overlooked for hundreds of years, but it has recently been rediscovered by nutritionists. According to the United Nations (UN) Food and Agricultural Organization (FAO), which coordinates a project for increasing the consumption of quinoa, the protein value of this cereal equals that of whole powdered milk. Quinoa usually grows at a high altitude, but it adapts easily to regions that have a considerable temperature difference between day and night, such as the Canadian prairies. It is easy to cultivate, in part because its seeds are covered with bitter saponin, which protects them from hungry birds and insects.

Quinoa's edible seed is defined as a pseudo-cereal and a pseudo oil-seed because of its unique nutritional profile, which is rich in fats as well as in carbohydrates Its protein content is twice that of other cereals. This protein has such an excellent amino acid balance that the National Academy of Sciences calls quinoa the "best source of proteins".

Nutritional value of quinoa

Calories	4,299 kcal/kg
Nutritious digestible part	93.7%
Proteins	15.4%
Starch	65.2%
Calcium	0.07%
Phosphorous	0.4%
Fats	8.75%
Fiber	3.64%
Ash	2.61%
Water	3.93%

The plant's small seeds are similar to millet, and they can be ground into flour and cooked in many different ways. Quinoa is often mixed with other ingredients. It can be eaten as a cereal for breakfast or turned into pasta. Quinoa can also be used in soups, stews, salads, and desserts.

Human beings need to take in proteins, fats, carbohydrates, minerals, vitamins, and water through food. These nutrients are contained in the meat of various animals (including fish) and in milk and other dairy products, as well as in eggs, most cereals, fruit, vegetables, and animal

Food Availability (kg per person/year - 1999)							
Food	Europe	Asia	Africa	North America	Central America	South America	Oceania
Cereals	130.6	173.8	146.5	112.7	163.5	111.1	85.4
Tubers and potatoes	93.7	46.3	131.4	66.8	16	67.8	91.1
Sugar or sweeteners	38.7	17.5	15.3	70.1	47.5	50.5	39
Pulses	2.6	5.3	8.7	4.8	10.9	10.9	4
Vegetable oils	16.1	8.4	8.4	25.4	10	12.7	16.2
Vegetables	112.5	116.2	52	125.2	50.5	47.8	98.7
Fruit	83	46.2	52.5	124.8	100.8	88.6	110.3
Drinks	88	13.8	29.7	101.9	37.3	43.9	90
Meat	70.5	26.4	15	120.2	47.8	64.3	91.2
Animal fats	11.1	2	0.7	7.5	3	2.8	6
Milk	206.9	41.6	35.3	255.1	101.5	116.3	199.9
Eggs	11.9	8.1	2.2	14.2	13.3	6.6	5.8
Fish	20.4	17.3	7.9	21.7	7.5	8.2	22.6

and vegetable oils. Meat consumption has quadrupled in the last 50 years, following a rise in incomes and an increase in population growth, particularly in urban areas. People living in industrialized countries eat four times as much meat as people who live in developing countries.

Population, income, and production and consumption of animal products										
Areas	Population (millions people) 2000	GDP/pers. on (US $) 2000	Production (thousands of tons/year, 1999 - 2001)				Consumption (kg/prers./year, 1999 - 2000)			
			Meat	Milk	Fish	Eggs	Meats	Milk	Fish	Eggs
Industrialized countries	940	27,680	105,000	348,000	32,000	76	77	197	27	12
Developing countries	5,155	1,230	131,000	237,000	94,000	4,083	27	45	9	7

Nutrients

Until the 20th century, not much was known about the content and nutritional value of food. As scientists began to understand the biological makeup of the different substances in food, however, they made considerable advances in food science and in medicine as a whole. Today, we know that a healthy diet must provide our bodies with proteins, fats, carbohydrates, minerals, vitamins, and water. We also know that nutritional requirements vary according to gender, age, climate, and activity.

The daily protein requirement for humans is about .04 ounces (1 gram) of proteins per 2.2 pounds (1 kilogram) of body weight. Children need more protein, however, and so do adults under certain conditions, such as during a pregnancy or while performing strenuous physical activities. Fats have a high calorie and energy content and help the body absorb certain vitamins. Carbohydrates are the most important resource in a person's diet, because they provide more than half of the daily required calories. Minerals help maintain cells, as well as a proper balance of salts and water. They are also involved in nerve and muscle activity, the synthesis of proteins, and the formation of bones and teeth. Finally, the body needs vitamins—in small amounts—to carry out some vital functions. Our bodies do not produce vitamins, so we have to get them through food.

Poor nutrition—which includes both overeating and undernourishment—is related to many diseases, in both industrialized and undeveloped countries.

The Seven Nutritional Groups

1	Meat, fish and eggs
2	Milk and other dairy products
3	Cereals, potatoes and derivatives
4	Pulses
5	Oils and cooking fats
6	Vegetables and fruit (with vitamin A)
7	Vegetables and fruit (with vitamin C)

Nutritionists have created seven different groups for the foods that we eat. Depending on a food's content and characteristics, as well as whether it is of animal or vegetable (plant) origin, it will fall into into one of these seven groups. No single food can provide all of the nutrients that we need, and a well-balanced diet will consist of foods from each of these seven categories.

Food Pyramids

A food pyramid is a graphic representation of a healthy, balanced diet. The pyramid shows the quantities of the various types of food that our bodies require. Complex carbohydrates (bread, cereals, rice, and pasta), which provide most of our calories, are at the base of the pyramid. Fruit and vegetables are next, followed by foods high in protein that are either of vegetable origin (legumes and dry fruit) or animal origin (meat, fish, and eggs). At the top of the pyramid are fats and sugars, which should be eaten in small quantities.

Fats, oils and sweets

Milk, yogurt and cheese

Meats, eggs, beans and dried fruit

Vegetables

Fruit

Bread, cereals, rice and pasta

Vitamin C

Ascorbic acid——more commonly known as vitamin C——is a water-soluble vitamin. It can be found in fruit and vegetables, but only if they are fresh and stored properly, because vitamin C is destroyed by light and heat. The foods richest in vitamin C are citrus fruits (such as oranges), wild fruits (berries, red currants, and black currants), sweet peppers, parsley, ripe tomatoes, potatoes, and green-leaf vegetables.

Vitamin C is one of the most effective antioxidants——it helps prevent the body's tissues from breaking down. It is vital for keeping our bones, teeth, and blood vessels healthy; it plays a crucial role in the healing of wounds and burns; and it helps the body absorb iron.

Most animals create vitamin C in their bodies. Humans, however, cannot create vitamin C, so they must get it from food. The daily requirement of vitamin C for adult humans ranges between .00004 ounces (1 milligram) to .00008 ounces (2 mg) per 2.2 pounds (1 kg) of body weight. For children, adolescents, or pregnant women, the daily requirement may be higher. In the past, a lack of vitamin C often resulted in scurvy, a potentially fatal disease that weakens blood vessels.

Oldways is an organization dedicated to promoting healthy diets. It has worked with leading scientists to develop a series of food pyramids that are based upon traditional diets in different parts of the world. These diets have proven to be effective for maintaining health and living a long life.

Compared to the United States Department of Agriculture (USDA) food pyramid, these Oldways pyramids, based on Asian and Mediterranean diets, recommend smaller amounts of meat, larger amounts of legumes, vegetables, and fruit, and no cooking fats that have animal origins.

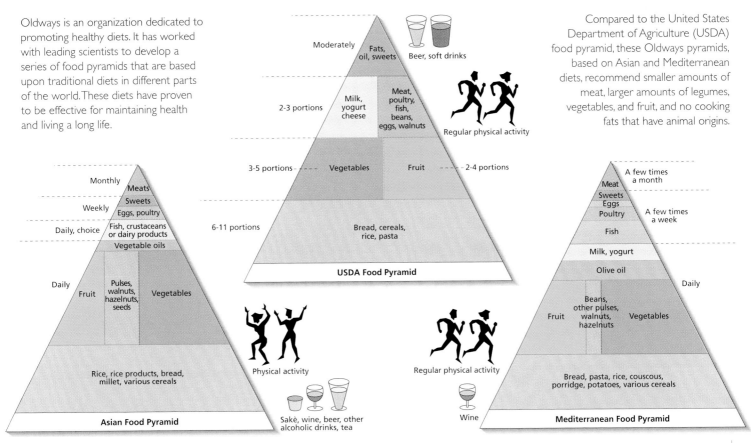

Asian Food Pyramid

Monthly — Meats
Weekly — Sweets
— Eggs, poultry
Daily, choice — Fish, crustaceans or dairy products
Vegetable oils
Daily — Fruit / Pulses, walnuts, hazelnuts, seeds / Vegetables
Rice, rice products, bread, millet, various cereals

Physical activity

Sakè, wine, beer, other alcoholic drinks, tea

USDA Food Pyramid

Moderately — Fats, oil, sweets / Beer, soft drinks
2-3 portions — Milk, yogurt cheese / Meat, poultry, fish, beans, eggs, walnuts
Regular physical activity
3-5 portions — Vegetables / Fruit — 2-4 portions
6-11 portions — Bread, cereals, rice, pasta

Mediterranean Food Pyramid

A few times a month — Meat
Sweets
Eggs
A few times a week — Poultry
Fish
Milk, yogurt
Olive oil
Daily — Fruit / Beans, other pulses, walnuts, hazelnuts / Vegetables
Bread, pasta, rice, couscous, porridge, potatoes, various cereals

Regular physical activity

Wine

Water
An Indispensable Resource

Water is the main component of almost all living things, including humans. We need water in order to survive. In addition to simply drinking it, we get water from other liquids and from food. Our bodies require about .8 gallons (3 liters) of water a day.

The human body uses water in many different ways. Water is vital for breathing and reproduction, for transporting hormones and vitamins in the body, and for regulating body temperature. It is the vehicle through which food is introduced into the body's cells. Water is directly involved in the synthesis, or joining together, of substances in the body, as well as in the breakdown of certain foods during digestion.

Since the 1960s, water consumption has increased at such a fast rate that freshwater—for drinking and for farming—is now becoming scarce in many parts of the world. This lack of water is partly due to the fact that the world's populations and its freshwater are not evenly distributed. Finding adequate supplies of freshwater will probably become a larger problem for future generations.

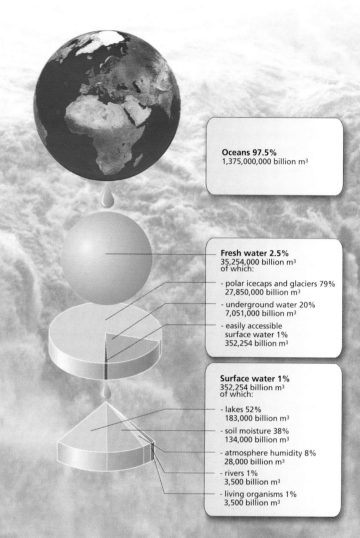

Oceans 97.5%
1,375,000,000 billion m³

Fresh water 2.5%
35,254,000 billion m³
of which:

- polar icecaps and glaciers 79%
  27,850,000 billion m³
- underground water 20%
  7,051,000 billion m³
- easily accessible
  surface water 1%
  352,254 billion m³

Surface water 1%
352,254 billion m³
of which:

- lakes 52%
  183,000 billion m³
- soil moisture 38%
  134,000 billion m³
- atmosphere humidity 8%
  28,000 billion m³
- rivers 1%
  3,500 billion m³
- living organisms 1%
  3,500 billion m³

Northern Europe
11,498

Eastern Europe
14,818

North America
16,801

Western Europe
2,215

Southern Europe
3,704

Eastern Asia
2,306

Central America
8,306

The Caribbean
2,640

Northern Africa
495

Western Asia
1,771

Western Africa
4,803

Central-Southern Asia
1,465

Southeast Asia
11,027

Central Africa
20,889

Eastern Africa
3,351

South America
36,988

Oceania
53,711

Southern Africa
1,289

Water availability
(yearly average in m³/pers.)

- less than 1,000
- 1,000-2,000
- 2,001-4,000
- more than 4,000

Water Scarcity in China

In 2001, reports by the Geological Environmental Monitoring Institute in Beijing, China, and by the World Bank sounded an alarm: the northern half of China is drying up. The lack of water, the World Bank forecast, will lead to "catastrophic consequences for future generations". This region produces more than half of China's wheat and one third of its corn. The pumping of water for farming, however, has emptied the layers of earth that hold water, leading to the drilling of deeper and deeper wells. In Hebei province, the average depth where water could be found dropped by 9.5 feet (2.9 meters) in 2000, and by as much as 19.7 feet (6 m) near the cities. Around Beijing, water is only found at a depth of 3,280 feet (1,000 m). In 1997, as many as 99,000 wells were

abandoned because they were dry, and 222,000 new ones were drilled. The flow of rivers, including the Yellow River, has decreased dramatically, and there are frequent periods of drought. Lakes are disappearing too: out of 1,052 lakes that once existed in Hebei province, only 83 are left. What will happen in 2010, when

the population of China is expected to have increased by 126 million people? The World Bank predicts that the demand for water all over the country will grow by 60 percent. Pumping costs will probably make water too expensive for farmers, which will certainly threaten China's food supply.

Supply of running water		
Year	Population not supplied	Population supplied through indoor plumbing
1990	3,107,000,000	2,159,000,000
2000	3,209,000,000	2,846,000,000

Water used for human consumption must meet certain physical, chemical, and bacterial requirements—for example, it must not contain more than 100 bacteria per 35 cubic feet (1 cubic meter). Today, natural water sources that meet these requirements are rarely found, especially

in urban areas or where agricultural and industrial activities are widespread. Pollution from these activities can seep down and contaminate the water-bearing layers. Surface waters (rivers and lakes) used for drinking can often become carriers of dangerous infections and disease.

Water that kills
Diseases caused by contaminated water

Cholera
(number of cases - 1999)
- less than 10*
- from 10 to 100
- from 101 to 1,000
- from 1,001 to 10,000
- more than 10,000
- * often these are imported cases

Guinea worm
cases identified (2000) ○

Trachoma
high number of cases ●

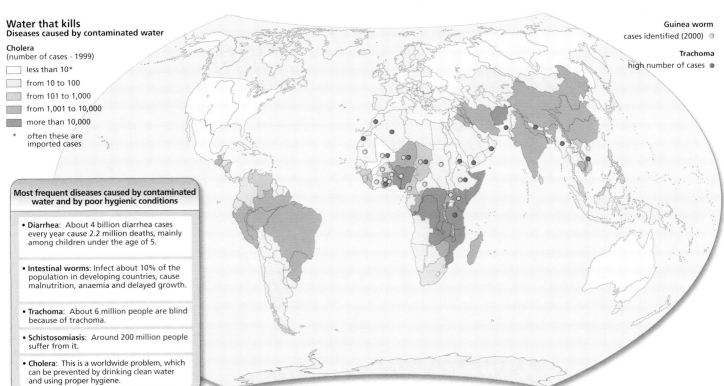

Most frequent diseases caused by contaminated water and by poor hygienic conditions

- **Diarrhea:** About 4 billion diarrhea cases every year cause 2.2 million deaths, mainly among children under the age of 5.

- **Intestinal worms:** Infect about 10% of the population in developing countries, cause malnutrition, anaemia and delayed growth.

- **Trachoma:** About 6 million people are blind because of trachoma.

- **Schistosomiasis:** Around 200 million people suffer from it.

- **Cholera:** This is a worldwide problem, which can be prevented by drinking clean water and using proper hygiene.

Origins of Agriculture
Domestication of Plants and Animals

The domestication of plants and animals is a fairly recent development in human history. Thousands of years probably went by before people made the connection between certain seeds and the plants that grew from those seeds. Environmental changes also had to occur before people could stop hunting and gathering and find alternative ways to get food: glaciers had to recede, climates had to become warmer, and plants that could provide people with large amounts of food—such as cereals and legumes—had to begin spreading.

About 13,000 years ago, the first agricultural settlements appeared. The settlements originated in four main regions: the "Fertile Crescent" (an area in modern-day Iraq and Iran), Southeast Asia, Central America, and the Andean region of South America. At the same time, the availability of extra food allowed people to domesticate certain animals that had previously been hunted, such as sheep, goats, pigs, and poultry. The spread of agriculture and animal breeding led to huge increases in food production, which helped fuel tremendous population growth. In regions where food was both plentiful and varied, people were able to count on the nutrition they needed.

North America
sunflower, mexican bea turkeys

Central America
avocado, cocoa, corn, american bean, pumpkin, sweet potato, tomato

South American
pineapple, yam

Andean Region
cotton, pumpkin, Lima b peanut, peppercorn, pot llama, Guinea pigs, alpacas

Early humans were nomadic hunter-gatherers who moved around in search of areas where food was available. At some point, groups of hunter-gatherers learned that certain plants reproduced periodically, and they settled in the regions where the plants grew. In these regions, they helped the plants spread by burning other vegetation.

Ways of obtaining food between 6000 and 4000 B.C.

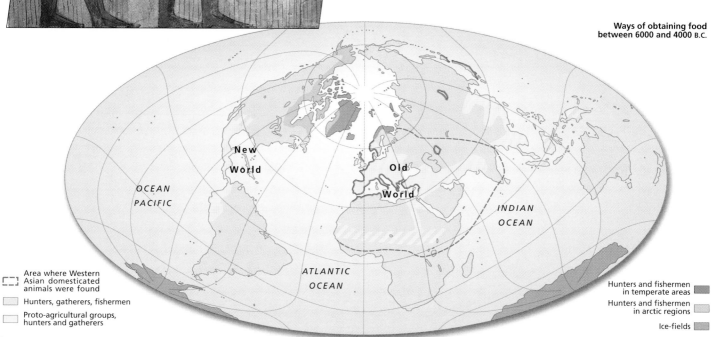

New World

Old World

OCEAN PACIFIC

INDIAN OCEAN

ATLANTIC OCEAN

Area where Western Asian domesticated animals were found

Hunters, gatherers, fishermen

Proto-agricultural groups, hunters and gatherers

Hunters and fishermen in temperate areas

Hunters and fishermen in arctic regions

Ice-fields

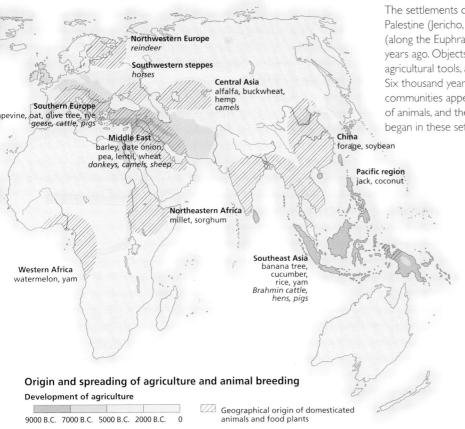

Northwestern Europe
reindeer

Southwestern steppes
horses

Central Asia
alfalfa, buckwheat, hemp
camels

Southern Europe
grapevine, oat, olive tree, rye
geese, cattle, pigs

Middle East
barley, date onion, pea, lentil, wheat
donkeys, camels, sheep

China
forage, soybean

Pacific region
jack, coconut

Northeastern Africa
millet, sorghum

Western Africa
watermelon, yam

Southeast Asia
banana tree, cucumber, rice, yam
Brahmin cattle, hens, pigs

The settlements discovered in Anatolia (Çatalhüyük), Palestine (Jericho, Beth Yerah), Egypt (Merinde), and Iraq (along the Euphrates river) date back 9,000 to 10,000 years ago. Objects found at the settlements include ceramics, agricultural tools, and the seeds of cultivated vegetable crops. Six thousand years ago, in large river valleys, new agricultural communities appeared. The use of plows, the domestication of animals, and the large-scale breeding of certain animals began in these settlements.

Hunter and gatherer populations in different environmental systems
(estimate on the biomass/theoretical population density ratio in a hunting/gathering area having a 10-km radius)

Environmental systems

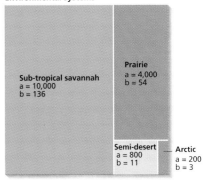

Sub-tropical savannah
a = 10,000
b = 136

Prairie
a = 4,000
b = 54

Semi-desert
a = 800
b = 11

Arctic
a = 200
b = 3

a = biomass in kg/km²
b = population per hunting/gathering area

biomass = number of living organisms which can be used as food

Origin and spreading of agriculture and animal breeding

Development of agriculture

9000 B.C.   7000 B.C.   5000 B.C.   2000 B.C.   0

Geographical origin of domesticated animals and food plants

focusON

Lactose Intolerance

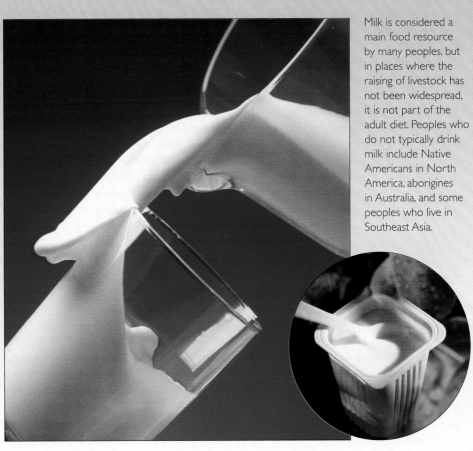

Lactose is a kind of sugar that is found in the milk of all mammals, including humans. In order to be absorbed into the body, lactose must be broken down into its two components, simple sugars called glucose and galactose. Lactose is broken down by an enzyme called lactase, which is found in cells that line the small intestine. Lactase is particularly active in babies, whose diet is mainly milk. In some cases, people are born without the ability to produce lactase, and disease or injury can also cause a lack of the enzyme. For most people, however, lactase decreases naturally after the age of two.

While some people who do not have a lot of lactase experience no problems when drinking milk, others do. These people are said to be lactose intolerant. When they drink milk, they experience nauseau, cramps, and other symptoms. Some people who are lactose intolerant avoid dairy products, while others take lactase supplements.

Milk is considered a main food resource by many peoples, but in places where the raising of livestock has not been widespread, it is not part of the adult diet. Peoples who do not typically drink milk include Native Americans in North America, aborigines in Australia, and some peoples who live in Southeast Asia.

The Spread of Agriculture

Vegetables were the first plants to be domesticated. Next, cereals were grown, followed by fruit trees and other useful plants (which provided timber, clothing, dyes, and medicines). The most important plants were cereals and legumes, which grow quickly, yield large amounts of food, and can be stored. These plants are sources of carbohydrates and proteins, and they led to the first human settlements and the development of great civilizations in various parts of the world. Wheat and barley in the Middle East, rice in Asia, and corn and beans in Central and South America all became the basic elements of the human diet. But an entire strip of Earth, between latitudes 10° south and 50° north, contributed to an increase in food resources at different times in history. Emmer (a kind of wheat) was first grown in a region that included parts of Europe, Asia, and the Middle East. Rye, broad beans, and oats were also grown in this region. Millet and sorghum come from Africa, while beans, potatoes, and tomatoes

come from tropical regions in the Americas. Commerce, migration, and exploration brought about exchanges of plants and animals. Plants from the New World spread to the rest of the planet, and animal species bred in the Old World were taken to the Americas.

The main animal species domesticated in ancient times		
Names	THE GREAT FIVES	Area of origin of their ancestor
Sheep		Central and Western Asia
Goat		Western Asia
Ox		Eurasia and Northern Africa
Pig		Eurasia and Northern Africa
Horse		Steppes in Southern Russia
	THE NINE LESSER ONES	
Camel		Arabia
Bactrian camel (two humped)		Central Asia
Llama and Alpaca		Andes
Donkey		Northern Africa and Middle East
Reindeer		Northern Eurasia
Asian buffalo		Southeast Asia
Yak		Himalaya
Domesticated Banteng		Indonesia
Mithan		India and Burma

Routes of people, goods, crops and animals in the Old World
(From Arab expansion -8th century- to the end of the 15th century)

Why not the Zebra?

Animals that are domesticated must have certain qualities that make them suitable for use by humans. Many animals do not possess such qualities, which is why, out of the many large animals that might make good candidates for domestication, humans have managed to domesticate only 14 of them. One of the most important characteristics for domestication is an agreeable temperament. Two equine species, for example, the horse and the ass (the domestic ass is called a donkey), have proven to be excellent domestic animals, useful and easy to handle. The horse, in particular, provided humans with a means of transportation

before the introduction of trains and automobiles. Other equine species, however, such as the zebra, have proven to be unsuitable for domestication.

Zebras are very similar to horses and donkeys, but they have a much more aggressive temperament that worsens as they get older.

Animal and plant exchanges between the Old and the New World

Between the mid-16th and the mid-17th century, many "botanical gardens" were created in Europe to host American plants

NORTH AMERICA

North America

Central America

Andean Region

South American Plain

PACIFIC OCEAN

LATIN AMERICA

ATLANTIC OCEAN

Northeastern Europe

Southern Europe

EUROPE

ASIA

AFRICA

Wheat, barley, rye, millet, oat, rice, sorghum, sugar cane, grapevines, olive trees, olive trees, coffee, fruit, cattle, sheep, pigs, geese, horses, hens, silkworms

Sunflowers, beans, avocado, cocoa, corn, potatoes, pumpkins, tomatoes, tobacco, peppers, peanuts, fine woods, peppercorns, turkeys, ducks, wool, alpacas, salmon, sweet potatoes, Guinea pigs

Geographical origin of food plants and domesticated animals

Pineapple	Pepper
Peanut	Tomato
Oat	Rice
Avocado	Rye
Cocoa	Tobacco
Coffee	Grapevine
Sugar cane	Pumpkin
Cotton	Alpaca
Bean	Cattle
Wheat	Horses
Sunflower	Llamas
Yam	Pigs
Corn	Geese
Olive tree	Guinea pigs
Potato	Reindeer
Sweet potato	Turkeys
Peppercorn	

Geographical origin of food plants and domesticated animals

Wheat and Rice

Wheat was originally a kind of wild grass. Along with grapevines and olive trees, wheat characterized the ancient Greek and Roman civilizations. Today, it is the most widespread cereal in the human diet. Wheat is rich in starch, cellulose, and proteins, as well as in vitamins E and B, sodium, potassium, calcium, and magnesium. Cultivated species of wheat can be divided into two groups: durum wheat and soft wheat. Durum wheat, rich in gluten, is used to make pasta and couscous. It needs sunlight and a dry climate, such as can be found in Sicily and northern Africa. Soft wheat, whose flours, rich in starch, are suitable for bread and sweets, comes in more varieties. It is the most widespread kind of wheat, particularly in temperate regions.

Rice was a good crop for the earliest farmers, since it grows underwater for most of the time and is therefore not affected by heavy rains or floods that often wash nutrients out of exposed soil. The cultivation of rice in paddy fields has been documented since the emergence of the Chinese civilization thousands of years ago. The species is divided into two main varieties. The Japonica variety, which has a short stem and round, lightly colored grains, is grown in China, Japan, Korea, and other subtropical regions. The Indica variety, which has a longer stem and elongated grains that remain separate even after cooking, is widespread in all Asian tropical areas.

Rice requires a warm, humid climate, and it needs higher temperatures and more limited temperature changes during the day than wheat. Rice crops produce more food than wheat crops, and this productivity has made it a staple diet in regions that are densely populated.

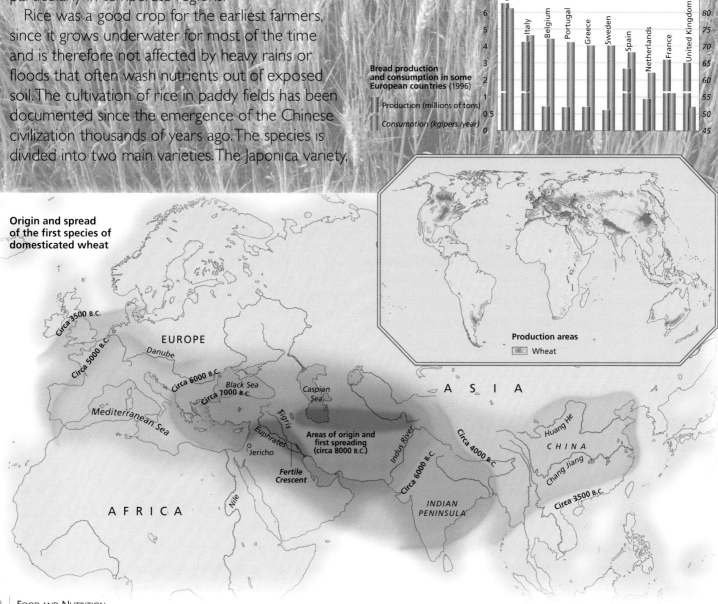

Bread production and consumption in some European countries (1996)

Production (millions of tons)

Consumption (kg/pers./year)

Origin and spread of the first species of domesticated wheat

Production areas
Wheat

Basmati Rice

Basmati rice is grown at the base of the Himalayas in India and Pakistan. It has a long grain that is transparent, white, or brown, and it typically has a nutlike taste. Basmati rice is considered to be one of the finest rice varieties in the world.

A few years ago, this rice became the center of a dispute that attracted international attention over the issue of "biopiracy." In 1997, a U.S. company, RiceTec, received a U.S. patent for a rice variety it had created, under the name basmati. The company claimed it had obtained the new variety by crossbreeding original varieties from India and Pakistan with other long-grain varieties. With this patent, the company could have demanded a share of the profits for any rice sold in the United States with the same qualities as its patented rice—even original basmati varieties. It would also have been able to market the variety worldwide as basmati rice. After India and Pakistan challenged the patent, some parts of

it were changed, and RiceTec can no longer use the basmati name.

Following this experience, the Indian government created a genetic database for several crop varieties that typically come from India. It also began urging organizations and countries to address the issue of biopiracy.

Basmati rice is an important export for India and Pakistan. India cultivates about 716,300 tons (650,000 metric tons) of basmati, in an area that represents 15 to 20 percent of the land on Earth that is used for rice crops. The country exports 65 percent to the Middle East, 20 percent to Europe, and 10 to 15 percent to the United States. Basmati rice is the most expensive rice variety on the international market.

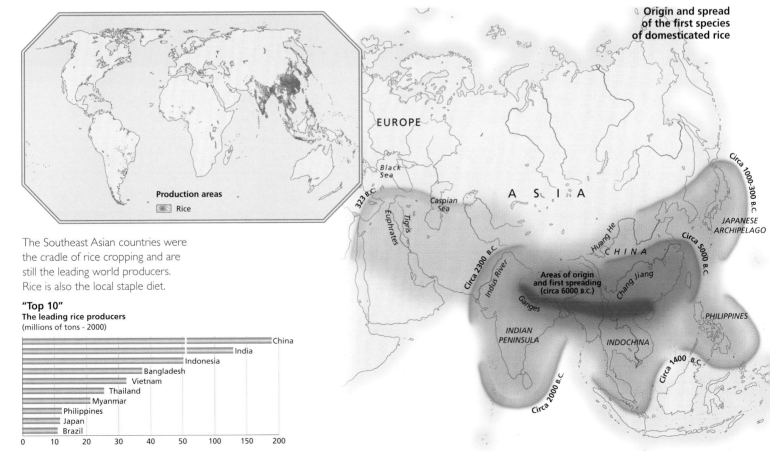

Production areas
- Rice

The Southeast Asian countries were the cradle of rice cropping and are still the leading world producers. Rice is also the local staple diet.

"Top 10"
The leading rice producers
(millions of tons - 2000)

China	~185
India	~130
Indonesia	~50
Bangladesh	~37
Vietnam	~32
Thailand	~25
Myanmar	~21
Philippines	~12
Japan	~11
Brazil	~10

Origin and spread of the first species of domesticated rice

Circa 1000–300 B.C.
JAPANESE ARCHIPELAGO
EUROPE
Black Sea
Caspian Sea
ASIA
323 B.C.
Euphrates
Tigris
Huang He
CHINA
Circa 5000 B.C.
Circa 2300 B.C.
Indus River
Areas of origin and first spreading (circa 6000 B.C.)
Chang Jiang
Ganges
PHILIPPINES
INDIAN PENINSULA
INDOCHINA
Circa 1400 B.C.
Circa 2000 B.C.

Other Important Crops

In addition to wheat and rice, other crops also play large roles in the human diet, both because they are widespread and because they provide edible seeds and leaves, flour, and oil. Corn (also called maize), for example, is a major cereal crop. Many people eat corn in the form of whole kernels, but it is also grown for the production of flour, starch, and oil. Barley is another important crop. Barley grains are used to make flour for bread, livestock feed, diet products, coffee substitutes, and alcohol (barley varieties that are low in gluten are used to brew beer). In some areas, people eat cooked barley grains. Sorghum is mainly used to feed cattle and poultry. Some Asian and African populations use sorghum to make bread, however, and it is a major part of their diets.

Peanut and soybean plants are two crops that are high in protein. Peanut seeds are used to make oil and butter, and peanut butter is especially popular in the United States. Flour made from soybean is used to make animal feeds, and soybean is also used in substitutes for meat and dairy products. In addition, soybean seeds make an excellent variety of oil. The soybean plant and its derivatives will probably play an increasingly crucial role in feeding the human population, given the imbalance of food distribution in the world and the need to find vegetable protein sources that are cheaper than animal sources. Potatoes are another important part of the human diet. In addition, they are widely used in the production of starch and alcohol.

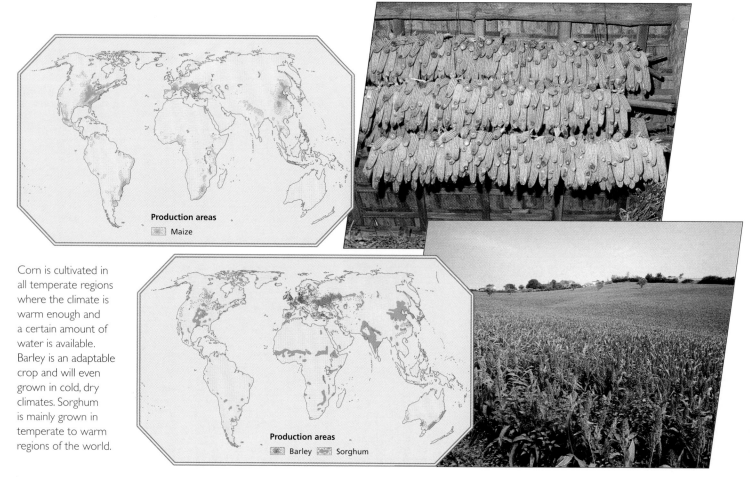

Production areas
▨ Maize

Production areas
▨ Barley   ▨ Sorghum

Corn is cultivated in all temperate regions where the climate is warm enough and a certain amount of water is available. Barley is an adaptable crop and will even grown in cold, dry climates. Sorghum is mainly grown in temperate to warm regions of the world.

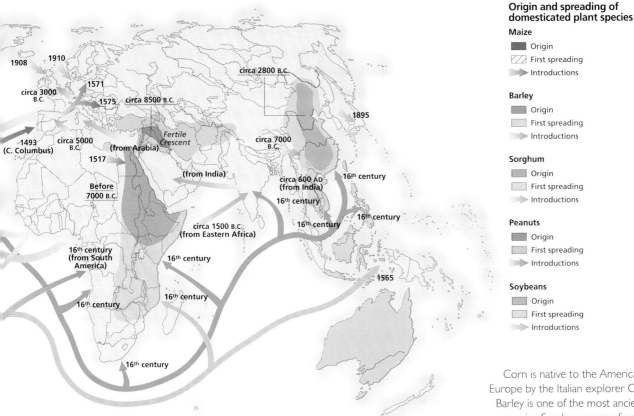

Origin and spreading of domesticated plant species

Maize
- ▓ Origin
- ▨ First spreading
- ➤ Introductions

Barley
- ▓ Origin
- ▢ First spreading
- ➤ Introductions

Sorghum
- ▢ Origin
- ▢ First spreading
- ➤ Introductions

Peanuts
- ▓ Origin
- ▢ First spreading
- ➤ Introductions

Soybeans
- ▢ Origin
- ▢ First spreading
- ➤ Introductions

1908
1910
1571
circa 3000 B.C.
1575
circa 8500 B.C.
circa 2800 B.C.
1895
1493 (C. Columbus)
circa 5000 B.C.
(from Arabia)
Fertile Crescent
circa 7000 B.C.
1517
(from India)
Before 7000 B.C.
circa 600 AD (from India)
16th century
16th century
16th century
16th century
circa 1500 B.C. (from Eastern Africa)
16th century
16th century
16th century (from South America)
16th century
16th century
1565
16th century
16th century
16th century

Potato plants are mostly found in temperate regions. They grow best in cool, humid climates and can be damaged by sudden temperature changes. The parts of the plant that are above ground are inedible, due to the presence of a toxic substance called solanine.

Corn is native to the Americas and was brought to Europe by the Italian explorer Christopher Columbus. Barley is one of the most ancient domesticated food species. Sorghum comes from Africa. Peanuts were brought to Europe (specifically Spain) from Brazil in the 1500s. The Portuguese brought them to Africa, and African slaves introduced them to North America. Soybeans come from the Asian Far East, Australia, and the Pacific islands. Potatoes are native to the Andes region of Peru and Bolivia. They were brought to Europe in the second half of the 16th century but were not grown on a large scale until the mid-18th century.

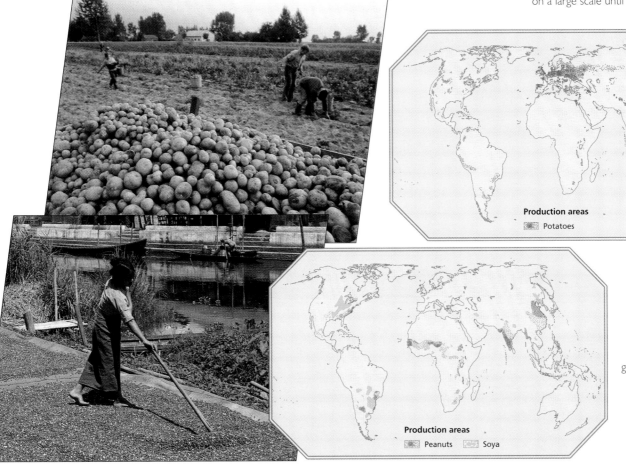

Production areas
- ▓ Potatoes

Production areas
- ▓ Peanuts   ▨ Soya

The highest peanut production is in India, China, West Africa, and the United States. Soybeans are grown for food, oil, and medicinal purposes in China, Japan, other Asian countries, and the United States, but mainly for oil in Europe.

Beverages

Beverages can be classified according to the amount of alcohol they contain. Non-alcoholic beverages contain less than 1 percent alcohol, and alcoholic beverages contain more than 1 percent. Soft, or non-alcoholic, drinks are created by mixing various substances with water. These substances include fruit juice, plant or herb extracts (coffee, tea, roselle, maté, and cocoa), powdered milk, flavors, and colors. In some countries, people drink bottled mineral water because of the poor quality of tap water, and in other countries, they drink it simply for taste or because it is fashionable. Fermented alcoholic beverages, such as wine and beer, are created through the action of microorganisms on sugary substances (grape must for wine, barley malt for beer, apple must for cider). In general, the alcohol content of fermented beverages does not exceed 16 percent per volume. Distilled alcoholic beverages are created when sugary substances are fermented and then distilled. The distillation process increases the alcohol content, and distilled alcoholic beverages typically contain between 38 and 60 percent alcohol per volume. Distilled alcoholic beverages are often aged in wooden casks. Some alcoholic beverages are created by mixing alcohol with aromatic herbs.

Like foods, beverages are often closely related to the particular environments where they are created, as well as to local traditions and habits.

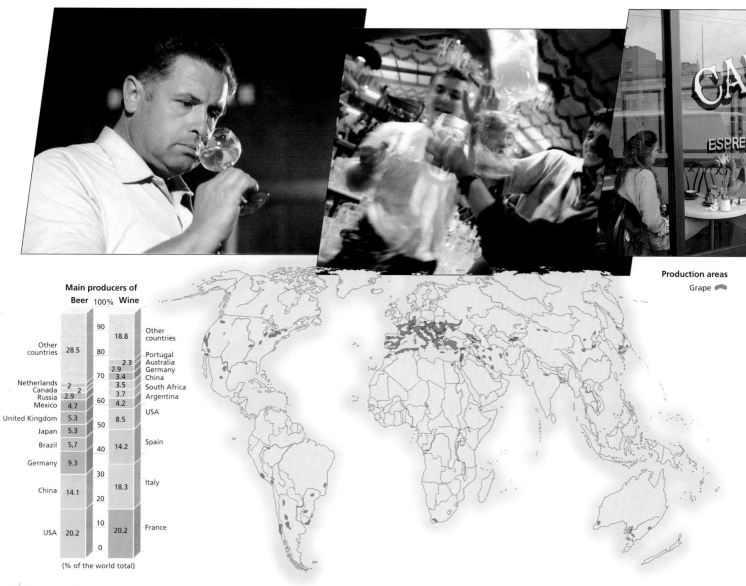

Production areas

Grape

Main producers of

Beer	Wine	
	100%	
	90	
Other countries 28.5	18.8	Other countries
	80	
	2.3	Portugal
	2.9	Australia
	3.4	Germany / China
Netherlands 2	70	
Canada 2	3.5	South Africa
Russia 2.9	3.7	Argentina
Mexico 4.7	60	4.2
		USA
United Kingdom 5.3	8.5	
Japan 5.3	50	
Brazil 5,7	40	14.2	Spain
Germany 9.3	30	
China 14.1	18.3	Italy
	20	
	10	
USA 20.2	20.2	France
	0	

(% of the world total)

Coca-Cola and Pepsi-Cola

Coca-Cola is a carbonated soft drink made of water, sugar, caramel, caffeine, and extracts of walnut and coca leaves. It was created in 1886 by a pharmacist from Atlanta, Georgia. In 1892, the Coca-Cola Company was established, and in 1906 it opened its first factories abroad, in Canada, Cuba, and Panama. Today, over 70 percent of the company's products are sold outside of the United States, and bottling plants are located around the world.

In the 1890s, a pharmacist from New Burn, North Carolina, created a beverage that was similar to Coca-Cola. It contained pepsin, an enzyme found in the stomach that helps digest food. Like Coca-Cola, Pepsi-Cola met with worldwide success, and eventually bottling plants were constructed in almost 200 countries.

Today, the Coca-Cola Company and PepsiCo dominate the soft drink market around the world. The two companies each offer many different brands of soft drinks, and they compete against each other through advertising campaigns and the introduction of new products.

Producing companies	Market shares (%)	Produced units
Coca-Cola Co.	43.7	4,376,700,000
PepsiCo	31.6	3,124,100,000
Others	24.7	3,468,500,000

Main producers of

Coffee 100% **Tea**

Coffee		Tea
Other countries	25.4	Other countries 10.7
		Argentina / Iran 1.7
		Vietnam 2.2
		Japan 2.6
		Indonesia 2.8
		5.3
Honduras	2.6	Turkey 6.0
Ethiopia	3.1	
India	3.9	Kenya 7.9
Guatemala	4.2	
Côte d'Ivoire	4.5	Sri Lanka 10.2
Mexico	4,6	
Indonesia	6.7	
Colombia	8.6	China 23.6
Vietnam	10.8	
Brazil	25.6	India 27.0

(% of the world total)

Production areas
Tea
Coffee

Agriculture Today
Different Methods

Agricultural methods differ in various parts of the world. In Europe and Asia, for example, intensive farming is practiced—farmers try to get the highest possible yield per acre, often from small amounts of land. In other regions, such as parts of Africa, extensive farming is practiced—the yield per acre is relatively low, and the crops are usually planted over a large area. The practice of extensive farming may be the result of poor soil, obsolete agricultural techniques, or the easy availability of arable land. In the United States, automated farm machinery and agricultural advances have resulted in high-yield crops planted over very large areas.

Today, agriculture can be divided into two main types: subsistence farming and commercial farming. The goal of subsistence farming is survival. Families (or even small communities) grow crops for food they can eat. This kind of farming is common in most poorer countries. The goal of commercial farming is profit. Commercial farms are businesses selling the crops they grow. This kind of farming is found in wealthy nations, as well as in poorer countries that have large plantations employing many workers. Some farmers own the land they cultivate, while others lease it. Farms may be owned by individuals or companies, but they may also be cooperatives, owned and run by a group of farmers.

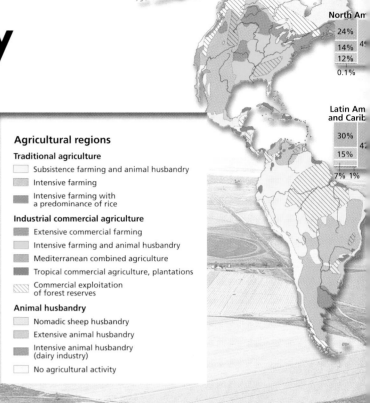

Agricultural regions

Traditional agriculture
- Subsistence farming and animal husbandry
- Intensive farming
- Intensive farming with a predominance of rice

Industrial commercial agriculture
- Extensive commercial farming
- Intensive farming and animal husbandry
- Mediterranean combined agriculture
- Tropical commercial agriculture, plantations
- Commercial exploitation of forest reserves

Animal husbandry
- Nomadic sheep husbandry
- Extensive animal husbandry
- Intensive animal husbandry (dairy industry)
- No agricultural activity

North Am
24%
14%   4
12%
0.1%

Latin Am
and Carib
30%
15%   4
7% 1%

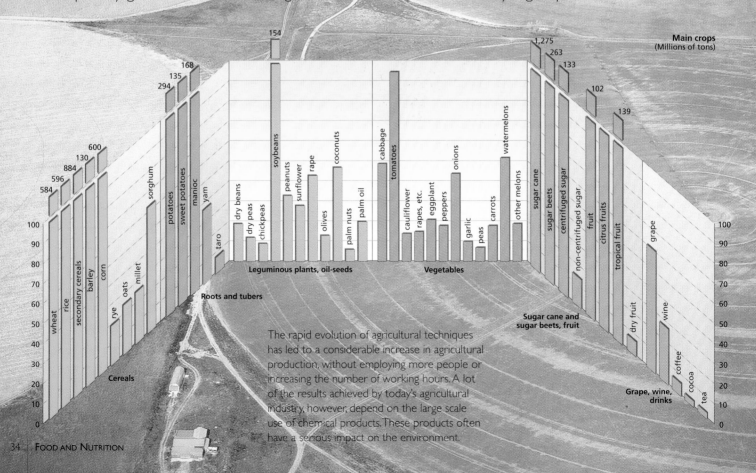

Main crops
(Millions of tons)

The rapid evolution of agricultural techniques has led to a considerable increase in agricultural production, without employing more people or increasing the number of working hours. A lot of the results achieved by today's agricultural industry, however, depend on the large scale use of chemical products. These products often have a serious impact on the environment.

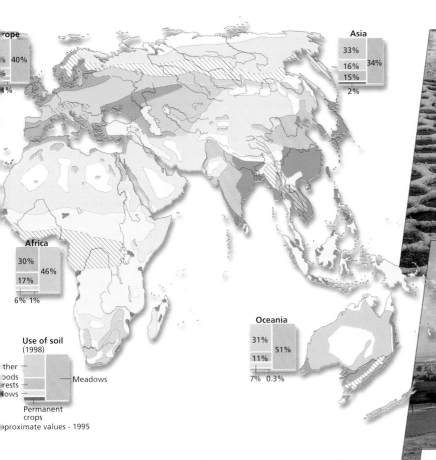

Europe
40%

Asia
33%
16%
15%
2%
34%

Africa
30%
17%
6% 1%
46%

Use of soil
(1998)
ther
ods
ests
ows
Meadows
Permanent
crops
proximate values - 1995

Oceania
31%
11%
7% 0.3%
51%

focus ON

Agricultural Reforms

Agricultural reforms attempt to improve the lives of people in rural areas. Such reforms may involve the redistribution of property, to ensure fair access to land and water, or the development of better farming methods, to increase productivity. From ancient Roman times, when war veterans were given farmland, to the French Revolution of the late 18th century, when land for farmers was confiscated from the wealthy nobility, agricultural reforms have been a part of history. In the 20th century, agricultural reform was a key issue for many political movements and revolutionary causes, with two of the most significant agricultural reforms occurring in the Soviet Union and China. In 1945, when the Food and Agriculture Organization (FAO) was established, it recommended agricultural reform as "one of the most effective tools to achieve rural transformation and agricultural development." The FAO also stated that individual governments should have the main responsibility for agricultural reform.

Since then, many countries have successfully carried out agricultural reform. In China, Laos, and Vietnam, such reforms have helped significantly in reducing poverty, while in South Korea, Japan, and Taiwan, they have helped support overall economic development.

Subsistence farmers usually rely on a few basic tools, and, occasionally, animals. Commercial agriculture, which includes greenhouses and large farms, involves advanced equipment and techniques, as well as considerable investments of money. This kind of agriculture fosters the creation of large companies and often inflicts a heavy toll on the environment. Since it does not require a lot of labor, it also speeds up rural depopulation.

Livestock and Fish

Animal husbandry, which is the care and breeding of livestock, or domestic animals, plays a large role in agriculture. In wealthy countries, it accounts for 70 percent of agricultural revenues. Some crops are raised just to provide livestock feeds.

Animal husbandry can be intensive or extensive. Intensive animal husbandry is widespread in the limited open spaces of Western Europe and in the regions of the United States that produce meat and dairy products. This kind of animal husbandry includes automated cattle sheds requiring a limited labor force, scientifically developed diets and feeding methods, and breeds that are specifically selected for certain desirable traits. Extensive animal husbandry is practiced in semi-wilderness areas and often involves moving animals around in scarcely populated regions. This kind of husbandry is widespread on the plains of North and South America and in areas of Russia. Its goal is usually the production of meat.

Ocean fishing represents the main source of subsistence for many peoples living in coastal areas, and it is a vital element in the economies of many countries. The use of large, powerful ships, fitted with refrigeration systems that allow long-term storage, has transformed the fishing industry. Traveling great distances on lengthy voyages, these ships catch a tremendous amount of fish.

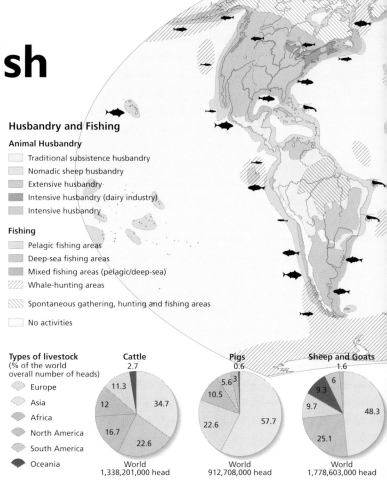

Husbandry and Fishing

Animal Husbandry
- Traditional subsistence husbandry
- Nomadic sheep husbandry
- Extensive husbandry
- Intensive husbandry (dairy industry)
- Intensive husbandry

Fishing
- Pelagic fishing areas
- Deep-sea fishing areas
- Mixed fishing areas (pelagic/deep-sea)
- Whale-hunting areas
- Spontaneous gathering, hunting and fishing areas
- No activities

Types of livestock
(% of the world overall number of heads)
- Europe
- Asia
- Africa
- North America
- South America
- Oceania

Cattle
2.7, 11.3, 12, 16.7, 22.6, 34.7
World
1,338,201,000 head

Pigs
0.6, 5.6, 3, 10.5, 22.6, 57.7
World
912,708,000 head

Sheep and Goats
1.6, 6, 9.3, 9.7, 25.1, 48.3
World
1,778,603,000 head

In addition to ocean fishing, close-range coastal fishing—which takes place up to 20 miles (32 km) from the coast—is still flourishing. Although it does not make use of advanced technological methods, it supplies many local markets with fresh fish. For some communities, fresh-water fishing is still very important, contributing to their survival.

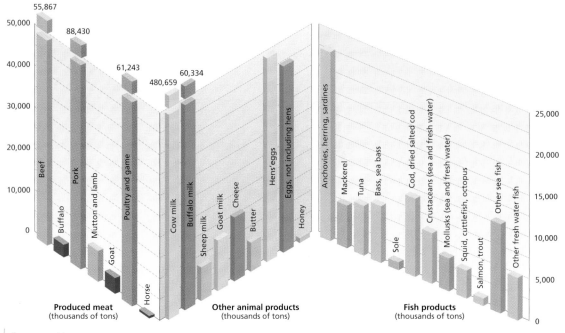

Produced meat (thousands of tons)
- Beef 55,867
- Buffalo
- Pork 88,430
- Mutton and lamb
- Goat
- Poultry and game 61,243
- Horse

Other animal products (thousands of tons)
- Cow milk 480,659
- Buffalo milk 60,334
- Sheep milk
- Goat milk
- Cheese
- Butter
- Hens' eggs
- Honey

Fish products (thousands of tons)
- Anchovies, herring, sardines
- Mackerel
- Tuna
- Bass, sea bass
- Sole
- Cod, dried salted cod
- Crustaceans (sea and fresh water)
- Mollusks (sea and fresh water)
- Squid, cuttlefish, octopus
- Salmon, trout
- Other sea fish
- Other fresh water fish

Today, poultry farming (or aviculture) has reached the same level of economic importance as cattle and pork farming. Aviculture is a highly automated activity in industrialized countries. It involves techniques to increase fertility and control feeding, and it relies on preventive medicine to protect against diseases. In the fishing industry, anchovies, herring, and sardines are the leading products.

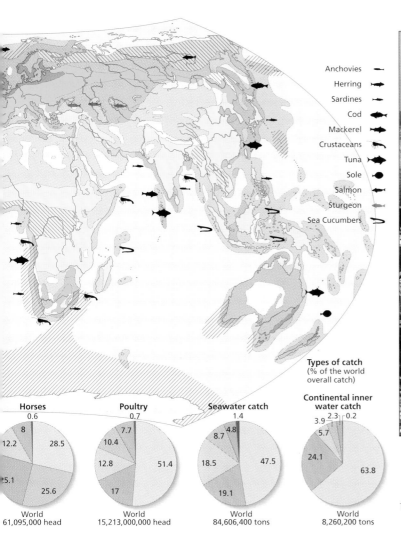

Anchovies
Herring
Sardines
Cod
Mackerel
Crustaceans
Tuna
Sole
Salmon
Sturgeon
Sea Cucumbers

Types of catch
(% of the world
overall catch)

Horses
0.6
8
12.2   28.5
5.1
25.6
World
61,095,000 head

Poultry
0.7
7.7
10.4
12.8   51.4
17
World
15,213,000,000 head

Seawater catch
1.4
4.8
8.7
18.5   47.5
19.1
World
84,606,400 tons

**Continental inner
water catch**
3.9 2.3 0.2
5.7
24.1   63.8
World
8,260,200 tons

Commercial fishing boats catch shoal fish, such as sardines, herring, and anchovies (together, they account for one third of the world catch) as well as tuna, mackerel, and fish living in colonies, such as cod. Slightly more than half of the world catch comes from the Pacific Ocean; over one-third comes from the Atlantic Ocean. Less than one-tenth overall comes from the Indian Ocean and the Mediterranean Sea.

Aquaculture

Fish farming, or aquaculture, involves the raising and breeding of fish. Aquaculture is practiced in artificial freshwater basins, lagoons, coastal ponds, and shallow sea areas. In the last few years, it has provided more than 20 percent of the world catch. Fish farmers usually raise species with a high commercial value. These species include bass, giltheads, mollusks, crustaceans, algae, eels, and freshwater fish such as trout, carp, and salmon. In aquaculture, science and technology play a big role, helping fish farmers select the most suitable species, prepare feeds, prevent epidemics that could wipe out fish populations, and keep the water clean. Aquaculture is an important part of the economy for several Asian countries.

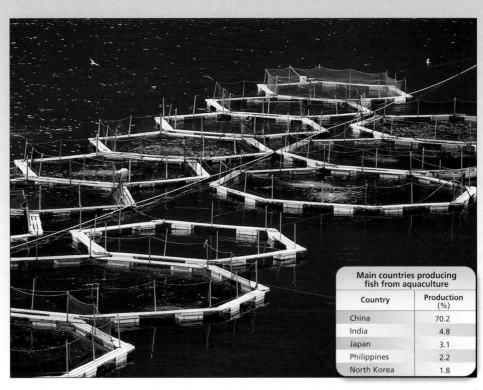

Main countries producing fish from aquaculture	
Country	Production (%)
China	70.2
India	4.8
Japan	3.1
Philippines	2.2
North Korea	1.8

Producing More Food
Innovative Methods and Techniques

In many regions of the world, people are going hungry. Rapid population growth has dramatically increased the demand for food resources and a more even distribution of those resources around the globe. Many countries will need to become more self-sufficient, producing larger amounts of food through more efficient methods.

Today, many agricultural innovations are being explored. These innovations seek to improve food production while reducing energy and labor costs. Current agricultural trends include new irrigation and fertilization techniques, the extensive use of pesticides, and large-scale mechanized farming. Computers now play a role in the agricultural industry. Farmers use computers in complex automated operations, such as the milking of cows. They also use computers to determine the best diets for certain animals or the most effective fertilization methods.

Another important agricultural advance is the creation of arable land through the construction of canals and dams. In the United States, for example, the waters of the Missouri River and its tributaries have been channeled to create thousands of acres of irrigated land, helping to lay the foundation for the country's considerable production capacity. Today, desert areas all over the world have been reclaimed for farmland. In Israel, the Negev desert has been turned into a farming region by channeling the Jordan River, desalinating sea water, and other measures. Land reclamation projects are expensive and are usually undertaken by wealthier nations. Poorer countries will need financial help for these kinds of projects.

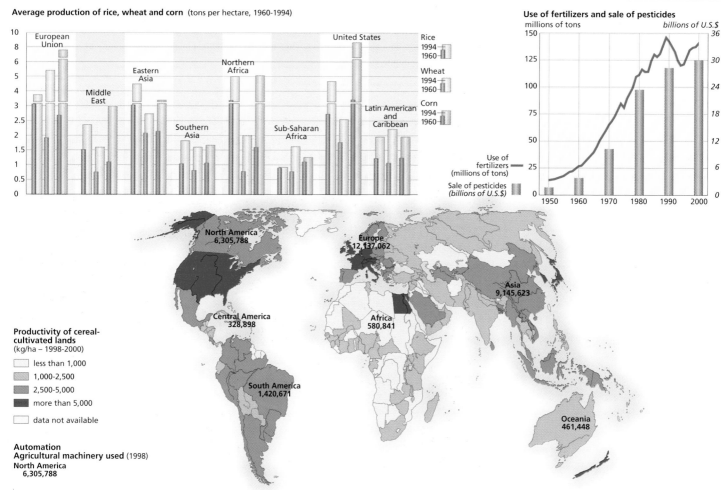

Average production of rice, wheat and corn (tons per hectare, 1960-1994)

European Union · Middle East · Eastern Asia · Southern Asia · Northern Africa · Sub-Saharan Africa · United States · Latin American and Caribbean

Rice 1994/1960 · Wheat 1994/1960 · Corn 1994/1960

Use of fertilizers and sale of pesticides
millions of tons — billions of U.S.$

Use of fertilizers (millions of tons)
Sale of pesticides (billions of U.S.$)

1950 1960 1970 1980 1990 2000

North America 6,305,788
Europe 12,137,062
Asia 9,145,623
Central America 328,898
Africa 580,841
South America 1,420,671
Oceania 461,448

Productivity of cereal-cultivated lands
(kg/ha – 1998-2000)
- less than 1,000
- 1,000-2,500
- 2,500-5,000
- more than 5,000
- data not available

Automation
Agricultural machinery used (1998)
North America 6,305,788

Cultivating the Desert

Water is the vital component that can transform desert soil into arable land. In some desert regions, people have had great success growing crops, with the help of an ancient system. This system was first used thousands of years ago in Persia, in what is now Iran. Known as *qanat* in Iran, the system consists of a network of tunnels that transports underground water to crops on the surface. This hidden, underground system prevents water dispersion and evaporation. Ancient qanat systems have been found in Egypt, Pakistan, and Sicily. In Iran, qanat networks can be thousands of miles long. Today, the system is often combined with new agricultural advances, such as basins to collect precious seasonal rain, seawater desalination plants, and wastewater treatment and recycling

Another agricultural innovation is a sprinkler, called a pivot, that moves in a giant circle. This circle can have a radius of almost 1,500 feet (450 m). Pivots are used extensively in the United States and the Arabian Desert, where they ensure up to ten harvests a year of lucerne, seven harvests of grass, and two harvests of corn. In Israel and the United States, drip-irrigation has been developed. Plants receive only the water they need directly from the roots, through drip systems or perforated hoses. This method does not require any special configuration of the land, ensures a high degree of accuracy in the water supply in all conditions, prevents the flow of water, and leaves the soil between rows of crops dry, so farmers can keep working. In particular, drip-irrigation systems dramatically limit water evaporation, resulting in water savings of between 30 and 60 percent.

In this satellite photograph of the Arabian Desert, circular fields irrigated by pivots dot the landscape. Pivots are connected to wells that have powerful pumping systems. The water is enriched with specific doses of fertilizers. A warm climate and the availability of water allow crops to be cultivated all year.

Drip-irrigation in Israel
(liter/kg product)

Water saving compared to traditional techniques						
Type of irrigation	Citrus fruit	Avocado	Bananas	Cotton	Apples	Potatoes
Traditional techniques (1970)	240	1,220	1,700	1,400	550	250
Drip-irrigation (1984)	200	800	650	1,000	250	100
Saving (%)	17	34	62	29	55	60

The Green Revolution

The "green revolution" refers to innovations in agriculture that originated in Mexico in the 1940s and were implemented in many industrialized countries after World War II. In the 1960s, international organizations, headed by the FAO, promoted the spread of the green revolution in less developed countries. These organizations sought to increase agricultural productivity and the availability of food and thus lessen poverty and malnourishment. Green revolution projects mainly involved countries in South and Southeast Asia, the Middle East, North Africa, and Central America, as well as the countries of Turkey and Mexico. The best results were achieved in India, Pakistan, and Thailand.

The projects did not involve a redistribution of land or radical changes in agricultural methods. Instead, they sought to increase crop yields per acre through the introduction of hybrid varieties of cereals with high yields and the extensive use of fertilizers and pesticides.

These measures did, however, create problems. The plants lost their original features once they reached the second generation, and high yields could only be ensured if fertilizers and pesticides were used. As a result, farmers were forced to buy seeds every year, as well as fertilizers and pesticides. They also had to buy farm machinery. Many farmers went into debt, and they eventually had to sell their lands and move to the cities.

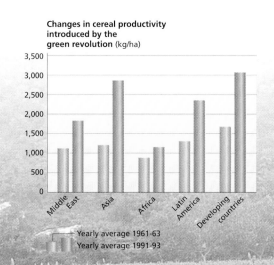

Changes in cereal productivity introduced by the green revolution (kg/ha)

Yearly average 1961-63
Yearly average 1991-93

The green revolution resulted in an increase in the yield per acre of cereals that are vital for nutrition, such as wheat, corn, and rice. The fast-ripening IR8 variety of rice, for example, can be harvested three times a year, and its yield is much higher than traditional varieties of rice.

The first green revolution
Industrialized countries (1950-1970)

The second green revolution
Developing countries (after 1967)

CGIAR agricultural research center

Gene banks

The Green Revolution in India

In India, the green revolution was extremely successful, leading to an increase in harvests and turning the country into one of the world's largest foodstuffs producers. Between 1947 and 1979, the yield per arable acre increased by 30 percent and the overall crop surface also grew.

Over time, however, the green revolution has resulted in negative consequences for both the environment and farming communities. The heavy use of chemical fertilizers—India is now one of the world's main consumers of these fertilizers—has caused pollution problems, while excessive irrigation has led to a high salt content in soils. Fewer varieties of plant species makes crops more vulnerable to parasite attacks and also results in fewer pulses, which are a precious source of protein in the nearly vegetarian Indian diet. In addition, only large companies in the northern regions of the country (Punjab, Haryana) were able to bear the high costs of technological innovations. Small land owners, meanwhile, went into debt and were forced to sell their lands. Starvation is a serious problem in India, where the poor cannot afford to buy the country's supplies of wheat and rice.

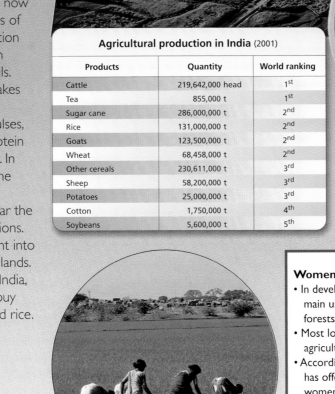

Agricultural production in India (2001)		
Products	**Quantity**	**World ranking**
Cattle	219,642,000 head	1st
Tea	855,000 t	1st
Sugar cane	286,000,000 t	2nd
Rice	131,000,000 t	2nd
Goats	123,500,000 t	2nd
Wheat	68,458,000 t	2nd
Other cereals	230,611,000 t	3rd
Sheep	58,200,000 t	3rd
Potatoes	25,000,000 t	3rd
Cotton	1,750,000 t	4th
Soybeans	5,600,000 t	5th

Some consequences of the green revolution in India
(1951-1992)

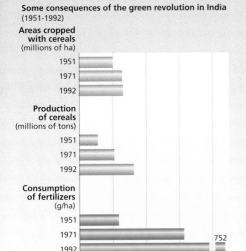

Areas cropped with cereals
(millions of ha)

1951
1971
1992

Production of cereals
(millions of tons)

1951
1971
1992

Consumption of fertilizers
(g/ha)

1951
1971 752
1992

0   100   200   300   400

Until a few decades ago, China and India were importers of rice and wheat respectively, but they have turned into exporters thanks to the green revolution. After their initial successes, however, these countries discovered that production could only be increased by using more fertilizers and pesticides. In developing countries, the use of fertilizers and pesticides has reached 55 pounds (25 kg) per 2.5 acres (1 ha).

Women and the Green Revolution
• In developing countries, women are the main users and managers of arable land, forests, water, and other natural resources
• Most low-income women depend upon agriculture to survive.
• According to the FAO, the green revolution has offered more benefits to men than to women (as well as more benefits to the wealthy than to the poor).
• According to the International Labor Organization (ILO), the implementation of new agricultural techniques "often implies the transfer of economic, employment and profit control from women to men."
• Agricultural automation in Bangladesh reduced female employment by 3.5 to 5 million working days per year.
• The introduction of machinery for rice shelling in Java eliminated the jobs of 1.2 million women, who had previously performed this activity manually and who owned no land.

Large Food Producers

In the last 50 years, there has been a remarkable increase in world food production. The United States ranks first in the world in the output of several agricultural products (such as corn and beef), thanks to its technological advances and its large areas of arable land. Food production levels in Canada and Australia are also high, but they are lower than in the United States, mainly because of climate. European agriculture mostly consists of small or medium-sized businesses, and only a few European products, including wine, oil, and some cereals, are sold on the international market.

Among the largest producers of rice are China and India. China's rice production has allowed it to become self-sufficient, while India produces enough rice to export it to other countries. Latin American countries are also involved in the international food market, breeding cattle and sheep and raising fruits and other specialized crops.

Despite the increase in world food production, food shortages are still a problem. Many African countries, for example, have large farms employing many people, but these countries suffer from a serious lack of basic food resources and cannot feed their growing populations. Russia, and other countries that belonged to the former Soviet Union, have large areas available for farming, but they cannot produce enough food and must rely on many imported items.

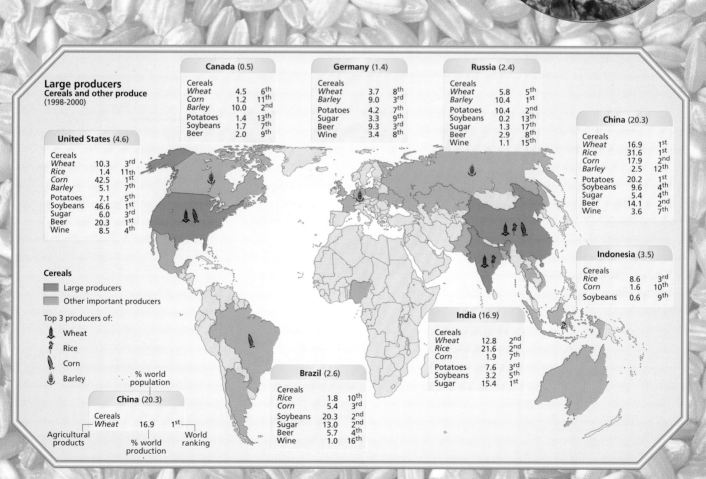

Large producers
Cereals and other produce (1998-2000)

Canada (0.5)

Cereals		
Wheat	4.5	6th
Corn	1.2	11th
Barley	10.0	2nd
Potatoes	1.4	13th
Soybeans	1.7	7th
Beer	2.0	9th

Germany (1.4)

Cereals		
Wheat	3.7	8th
Barley	9.0	3rd
Potatoes	4.2	7th
Sugar	3.3	9th
Beer	9.3	3rd
Wine	3.4	8th

Russia (2.4)

Cereals		
Wheat	5.8	5th
Barley	10.4	1st
Potatoes	10.4	2nd
Soybeans	0.2	13th
Sugar	1.3	17th
Beer	2.9	8th
Wine	1.1	15th

United States (4.6)

Cereals		
Wheat	10.3	3rd
Rice	1.4	11th
Corn	42.5	1st
Barley	5.1	7th
Potatoes	7.1	5th
Soybeans	46.6	1st
Sugar	6.0	3rd
Beer	20.3	1st
Wine	8.5	4th

China (20.3)

Cereals		
Wheat	16.9	1st
Rice	31.6	1st
Corn	17.9	2nd
Barley	2.5	12th
Potatoes	20.2	1st
Soybeans	9.6	4th
Sugar	5.4	4th
Beer	14.1	2nd
Wine	3.6	7th

Indonesia (3.5)

Cereals		
Rice	8.6	3rd
Corn	1.6	10th
Soybeans	0.6	9th

India (16.9)

Cereals		
Wheat	12.8	2nd
Rice	21.6	2nd
Corn	1.9	7th
Potatoes	7.6	3rd
Soybeans	3.2	5th
Sugar	15.4	1st

Brazil (2.6)

Cereals		
Rice	1.8	10th
Corn	5.4	3rd
Soybeans	20.3	2nd
Sugar	13.0	2nd
Beer	5.7	4th
Wine	1.0	16th

Cereals
- Large producers
- Other important producers

Top 3 producers of:
- Wheat
- Rice
- Corn
- Barley

% world population

China (20.3)

Cereals		
Wheat	16.9	1st

Agricultural products — % world production — World ranking

Whale Hunting

Whale hunting was once widespread because it was a very profitable activity. Valuable whale oil and whalebone had many uses, and parts of the whale could be made into products such as feeds and fertilizers.

By the 20th century, commercial whaling benefited from many advances in whale hunting. Echo sounders and aircraft could spot whales, ultrasound equipment could frighten them, and harpoons with explosives attached to the tips could kill them. Advances in whaling led to more whales being killed and eventually threatened some species with extinction. Blue whales, for example, were once abundant, but today only a few thousand are left.

Since 1946, the International Whaling Commission (IWC) has sought ways to protect whales. It banned commercial hunting in 1986 and put a total ban on some species, mothers with babies, and whales under a certain size.

Denmark — Norway — Japan

Hunting areas
Main whale-hunting countries

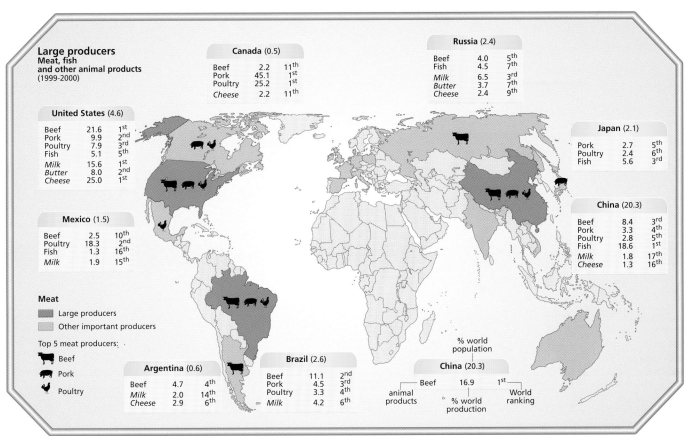

Large producers
Meat, fish and other animal products
(1999-2000)

Canada (0.5)

Beef	2.2	11th
Pork	45.1	1st
Poultry	25.2	1st
Cheese	*2.2*	*11th*

Russia (2.4)

Beef	4.0	5th
Fish	4.5	7th
Milk	*6.5*	*3rd*
Butter	*3.7*	*7th*
Cheese	*2.4*	*9th*

United States (4.6)

Beef	21.6	1st
Pork	9.9	2nd
Poultry	7.9	3rd
Fish	5.1	5th
Milk	*15.6*	*1st*
Butter	*8.0*	*2nd*
Cheese	*25.0*	*1st*

Japan (2.1)

Pork	2.7	5th
Poultry	2.4	6th
Fish	5.6	3rd

Mexico (1.5)

Beef	2.5	10th
Poultry	18.3	2nd
Fish	1.3	16th
Milk	*1.9*	*15th*

China (20.3)

Beef	8.4	3rd
Pork	3.3	4th
Poultry	2.8	5th
Fish	18.6	1st
Milk	*1.8*	*17th*
Cheese	*1.3*	*16th*

Meat

■ Large producers
□ Other important producers

Top 5 meat producers:

🐄 Beef
🐖 Pork
🐓 Poultry

Argentina (0.6)

Beef	4.7	4th
Milk	*2.0*	*14th*
Cheese	*2.9*	*6th*

Brazil (2.6)

Beef	11.1	2nd
Pork	4.5	3rd
Poultry	3.3	4th
Milk	*4.2*	*6th*

% world population

China (20.3)

Beef — 16.9 — 1st

animal products — % world production — World ranking

World Food Trade

The flow of food around the world is influenced by many factors. These factors include the distribution of cultivated lands, differing levels of productivity, specialization of crops, and different food habits in various regions of the world. In wealthier, developed countries, people consume large amounts of certain foods (wheat, fruit, vegetables, and meat) and want seasonal produce all year. Demand for these foods helps boost agricultural trade and production.

In the temperate regions of North America, production levels of staple foods such as wheat and corn are very high, and these foods are exported to the rest of the world. Other foods flow from developing countries to wealthy countries. In particular, tropical products (coffee, tea, cocoa, fruit, sugar, and plants used to make oil) move from Africa, Asia, and Latin America to industrialized countries. The sales of these foods are usually vital to the developing countries producing them, because the countries often have economies that depend on the export of one agricultural product. A decrease in demand for a certain product, or a drop in its price in wealthy countries, can cause a serious economic crisis for the developing country exporting it.

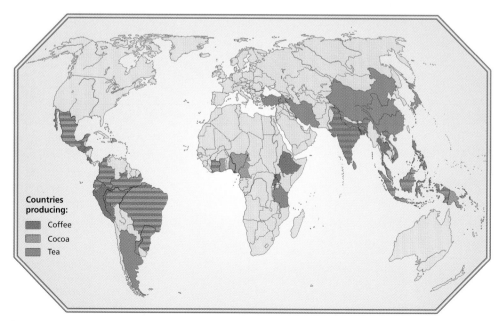

Countries producing:
- Coffee
- Cocoa
- Tea

Cereal export flows

- United States
- France
- Argentina
- Canada
- Australia
- Germany
- Thailand
- Kazakhstan
- United Kingdom
- ● Cereal exports in millions of tons (2000)

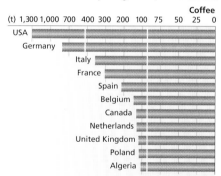

Main countries importing Coffee, Cocoa and Tea

Coffee

(t) 1,300 1,000 700 400 300 200 100 75 50 25 0

- USA
- Germany
- Italy
- France
- Spain
- Belgium
- Canada
- Netherlands
- United Kingdom
- Poland
- Algeria

Cocoa

(t) 400 300 200 100 75 50 25 0

- Netherlands
- USA
- Germany
- United Kingdom
- Belgium
- Italy
- Russia
- Brazil

Tea

(t) 100 75 50 25 0

- Russia
- Pakistan
- USA
- Egypt
- Japan
- Morocco
- Germany
- Poland
- Netherlands
- Saudi Arabia

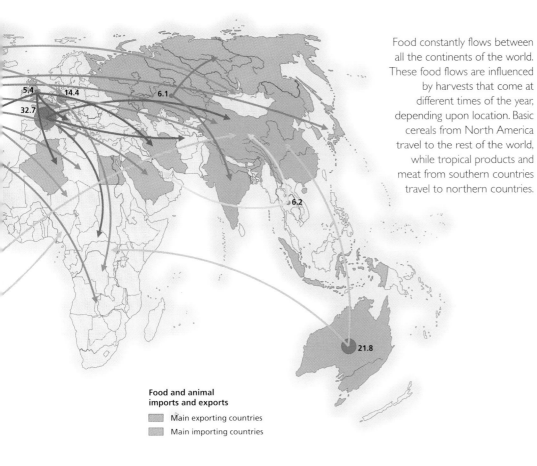

Food constantly flows between all the continents of the world. These food flows are influenced by harvests that come at different times of the year, depending upon location. Basic cereals from North America travel to the rest of the world, while tropical products and meat from southern countries travel to northern countries.

Food and animal imports and exports

- Main exporting countries
- Main importing countries

Fair Trade

Since the 1970s, developing countries that rely heavily on the export of tropical food products have been hit by a constant decline in the prices of those products. Today, for example, the price of coffee has decreased by as much as one fifth of its price from three years ago, causing many farm laborers and small farmers to suffer. These farmers cannot do much to change the situation, because 40 percent of the world's coffee is purchased and processed by four large, multinational companies that have a huge influence on coffee prices.

In Europe, a fair trade system was set up in the 1970s to combat inequalities found in international markets. This system seeks to establish equal trade relations between wealthy, industrialized nations and poorer, developing countries. The principles of fair trade include the direct import of products from developing countries, the setting of fair prices, advanced payment for goods, and giving preference to products sold by independent groups and cooperatives.

Over the last thirty years, farmers and craftspeople from Africa, Asia, and Latin America have come into contact with European fair trade organizations. Today, about 3,000 businesses that apply free trade principles can be found in over a dozen European countries.

North America, which includes the United States and Canada, is the top producer of wheat and corn. Worldwide demand for these cereals helps keep their prices high.

Rice is mainly grown in Asian countries. Some of these countries, such as India, produce enough rice to export, thanks to the green revolution. The trade in meat products is largely dependent on whether livestock are raised on feed or on grazing pastures.

EXPORT - IMPORT

Main countries exporting...		Main countries importing...	
Wheat (millions of tons - 2000)			
United States	27.8	Brazil	7.5
Canada	18.8	Italy	6.9
France	18.0	Iran	6.6
Australia	17.7	Japan	5.8
Argentina	11.0	Algeria	5.4
Kazakhstan	5.0	Egypt	5.0
Germany	4.6	Indonesia	3.6
Corn (millions of tons - 2000)			
United States	48.0	Japan	16.1
Argentina	10.8	South Korea	8.7
China	10.5	Mexico	5.3
France	7.9	Egypt	5.1
Hungary	1.0	Spain	3.5
		Malaysia	2.3
		Brazil	1.8
Rice (millions of tons - 2000)			
Thailand	6.1	Indonesia	1.4
Vietnam	3.5	Iraq	1.2
China	3.1	Iran	1.1
United States	2.7	Saudi Arabia	0.9
Pakistan	2.0	Nigeria	0.8
India	1.5		
Italy	0.7		
Barley (millions of tons - 2000)			
Germany	6.1	Saudi Arabia	5.3
France	4.8	China	2.1
Australia	3.0	Japan	1.7
Canada	1.8	Belgium	1.2
United Kingdom	1.6	Iran	1.0
United States	1.1	Morocco	0.9
Ukraine	0.9	Italy	0.7
Soybeans (millions of tons - 2000)			
United States	27.1	China	12.7
Brazil	11.5	Netherlands	5.4
Argentina	4.1	Japan	4.8
Paraguay	1.8	Mexico	4.0
Canada	0.8	Germany	3.8
		Spain	2.6
		South Korea	1.5
Meat (millions of tons - 2000)			
United States	5.0	Japan	2.4
Netherlands	2.0	United Kingdom	1.4
Denmark	1.5	Russia	1.3
Brazil	1.4	Italy	1.3
Australia	1.4	China	1.3
Belgium	1.2	Mexico	1.2
Canada	1.1		
Fish (thousands of tons - 2000)			
Norway	462	Japan	389
China	347	Denmark	369
Sweden	277	Spain	266
Indonesia	157	Italy	144
Thailand	156	Côte d'Ivoire	108
Canada	147	United Kingdom	84
Russia	140	Iceland	72

Agribusiness

The term agribusiness refers to industries that are involved in agricultural production. These industries provide farm machinery, pesticides and fertilizers, food processing, food additives and preservatives, and the transportation and distribution of products. Agribusinesses also include biotechnology companies, research institutes, and banks. The raising of crops and livestock is only a small part of agribusiness. In the United States, for example, 20 percent of the workforce can be found in agribusiness, but only 3 percent are directly employed in agricultural operations.

Today, industrial processes are used for the preparation of many kinds of foods. These operations are mostly handled by multinational companies that sell to very large markets. The companies often control all aspects of production, including the raising and harvesting of crops, food processing, and sales. They decide what crops should be grown and use advertising to influence what kinds of foods people consume.

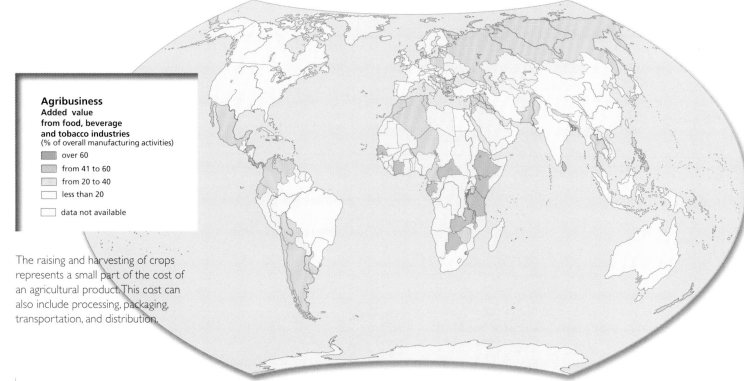

Agribusiness
Added value
from food, beverage
and tobacco industries
(% of overall manufacturing activities)

- over 60
- from 41 to 60
- from 20 to 40
- less than 20

- data not available

The raising and harvesting of crops represents a small part of the cost of an agricultural product. This cost can also include processing, packaging, transportation, and distribution.

Nestlé: A Multinational Food Corporation

In 1866, a German named Henri Nestlé established the Nestlé company to sell a milk-based product he had created specifically for babies.

In 1905 Nestlé, which by then had expanded considerably, merged with Anglo Swiss Condensed Milk Co., the most important European company producing condensed milk. In the years that followed, a series of mergers and takeovers would turn Nestlé into the world's leading food corporation, with a remarkably broad range of products.

Today, Nestlé's sales revenues can be divided as follows: 28 percent from mineral water and other beverages; 27 percent from milk-based and diet products; 25 percent from ready meals, culinary specialities, and pet food; and 13 percent from chocolate and other sweets. The rest of the company's revenues come from the sale of pharmaceutical products.

Nestlé owns more than 8,000 food and beverage brands. These brands, many of which are internationally famous, include Nescafe, Nesquik,

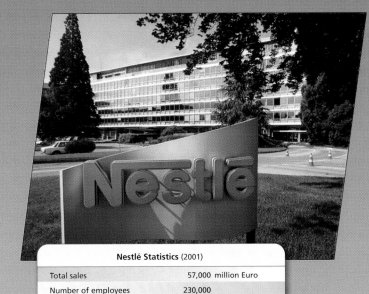

Nestlé Statistics (2001)	
Total sales	57,000 million Euro
Number of employees	230,000
Number of plants	468
Countries of operation	84
Sales abroad	60% of the total

KitKat, Smarties, Perrier, LCI, San Pellegrino, Buitoni, and Perugina. The company has been criticized for its questionable strategies aimed at getting local populations in developing countries to buy its products, particularly breast milk substitutes for babies .

In 1938, after many years of research, Nestlé introduced the world's first instant coffee. Called Nescafe, it was a powder that could be made into coffee by mixing it with water. Since its introduction, Nescafe has been a big success. The symbol for the Nestlé company is a small nest, which is recognized all over the world.

Agribusiness is dominated by the United States, which has the largest agribusiness companies and the highest number of them. U.S. companies control most of the world agribusiness trade, including the production of other large exporting countries, such as Canada, Brazil, and Argentina.

"Top 20"
Leading agro-industrial companies

Group	Country	Sector	Business volume (millions of US$)
Philip Morris	United States	Diversified production	53,288
Cargill	United States	Cereal processing	50,000
Nestlé	Switzerland	Diversified production	40,247
Pepsico	United States	Beverages	28,472
Unilever	Netherlands	Diversified production	26,150
Coca Cola	United States	Diversified production	23,828
Conagra	United States	Diversified production	23,512
RJB Nabisco	United States	Beer	15,366
Danone (BSN)	France	Diversified production	12,843
Anheuser Bush	United States	Diversified production	11,364
Grand Metropolitan	United Kingdom	Diversified production	11,300
Snow Brand Milk Products	Japan	Dairy products	10,600
Archer Daniels Midland	United States	Vegetable oils and fats	10,344
Bunge y Born	Argentina	Cereal processing	9,500
Maruha (Taiyo Fishery)	Japan	Fishing	9,221
Eridania/Beghin-Say	Italy	Vegetable oils and fats	9,157
Kirin Brewery	Japan	Beer	9,020
George Weston Ltd.	Canada	Food distribution	8,939
General Mills	United States	Diversified production	8,517
Allied Domecq Plc.	United Kingdom	Wines and spirits	8,375

World Market Concentrations in Agribusiness
- **Pesticides:** Five companies control 60 percent of the world market.
- **Genetically Modified Seeds:** Five companies control the world market.
- **Cereals:** Five companies control 75 percent of the world market.
- **Tropical Products:** A few multinational companies control 90 percent of the world trade in cocoa and pineapple, 80 percent in coffee and tea, 70 percent in bananas, and more than 60 percent in sugar.
- **Meat:** In the United States, four companies produce 80 percent of the country's beef and 60 percent of its pork.
- **Animal Husbandry:** In the United States, one third of beef comes from 70 farms, and poultry comes from farms raising over 100,000 heads per year. The number of pig farms has decreased by 72 percent, but the number of pigs bred has increased by 18 percent.

Economic Problems
Dependence of Developing Countries

Agricultural practices often play a central role in the problems facing many of the world's developing countries. In these countries, small-scale farming, which usually involves traditional methods that are not very productive, coexists with large-scale commercial farming. Small farms support local populations, but the main purpose of large commercial farms, which are very productive, is to provide exports to wealthy, developed countries. A developing country relying on such exports often gets trapped in a vicious cycle, becoming dependent on developed nations for both income and food.

Giant companies usually control these large-scale commercial farms, which practice monoculture—the cultivation of a single crop. The companies look for a developing country that has the right conditions for growing a certain crop. With cheap labor and land, as well as incentives from officials eager for new business, the companies make large profits.

This kind of farming, however, has drawbacks. It is based on an unfair distribution of land; it requires the purchase of equipment and materials that can increase a country's debt; and it limits farming to the most profitable crops, leaving few areas for the cultivation of other crops, which can support local populations. In addition, the developing countries have to rely on demand for their export crops in developed countries. The developed countries also set prices for the crops, as well as the cost of purchase and distribution.

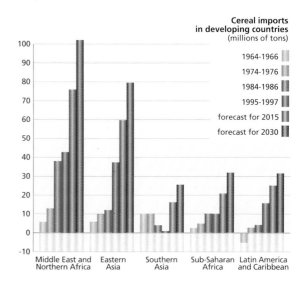

Cereal imports in developing countries (millions of tons)

1964-1966
1974-1976
1984-1986
1995-1997
forecast for 2015
forecast for 2030

Middle East and Northern Africa | Eastern Asia | Southern Asia | Sub-Saharan Africa | Latin America and Caribbean

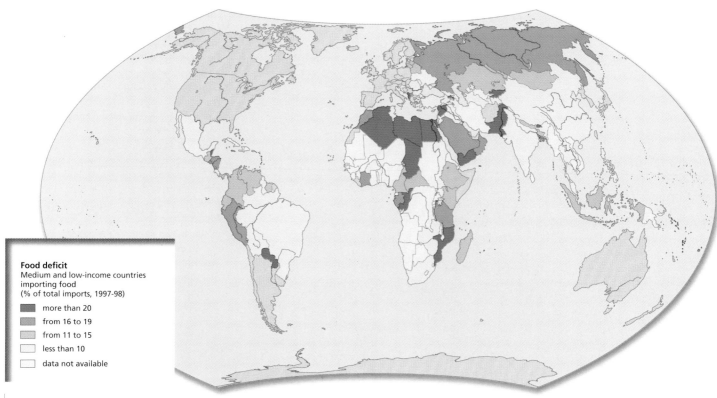

Food deficit
Medium and low-income countries importing food
(% of total imports, 1997-98)

- more than 20
- from 16 to 19
- from 11 to 15
- less than 10
- data not available

Monoculture: Sugar Cane in Cuba

Cuba is a good example of a country that has suffered from its reliance on one main crop export. In Cuba, one third of the arable land is devoted to the monoculture of sugar cane.

Before Cuba's leader, Fidel Castro, rose to power in 1959, Cuba exported sugar and rum (an alcoholic beverage made from sugar cane) to the United States and other countries. In 1960, however, the United States established an embargo against Cuba, ending all trade between the two countries. Cuba then established special relations with the Soviet Union, to which it sold sugar in exchange for oil, as well as technical and military support.

After the fall of the Soviet Union in 1991, however, Cuba's dependence on sugar had dramatic consequences. The country faced a drop in sugar prices and the loss of its main trading partner, which had provided it with industrial products, fuel, and foodstuffs in exchange for sugar.

By exchanging sugar for oil with the Soviet Union, Cuba was able to boost development, but the country also limited itself to an economy based on sugar cane. Cuba's other main crops—tobacco, coffee, and fruit—are also exported.

Production and exports of cane sugar in Cuba
(millions of tons)

production — exports

Monocultures and dependence on exports
(% of the individual countries' total exports)

Sugar		Cocoa		Coffee and surrogates		Tea and Mate	
Cuba	48.5	Sâo Tomé and Príncipe	75.0	Burundi	78.6	Kenya	27.0
Guyana	25.2	Côte d'Ivoire	37.0	Ethiopia	71.1	Burundi	14.2
Dominican Rep.	23.5	Ghana	25.2	Uganda	55.8	Sri Lanka	13.3
Mauritius	21.5	Dominican Rep.	8.5	Rwanda	31.2	Tanzania	5.5
Fiji	20.7			Nicaragua	25.9		
				Guatemala	23.4		
				El Salvador	21.2		
				Honduras	20.8		
				Tanzania	20.3		

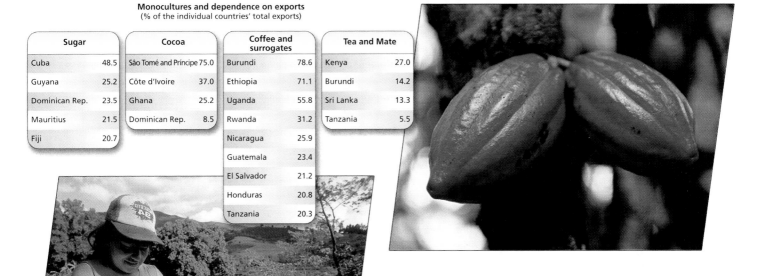

After the Spanish exploration of the Americas, cocoa—already known to the Mayas and the Aztecs—became popular in Europe. Indigenous and African slaves who were forced to cultivate cocoa—as well as cotton, sugar, and coffee—suffered badly.

Coffee is native to Africa, but it was brought to the Americas in the 1700s by European colonial powers, who established large coffee plantations. It is still a main crop and export product in many Latin American countries.

Science and Agriculture

Since agriculture first emerged, people have been trying to improve what they grow. Early farmers selected the best seeds and most suitable soils and made sure their fields were cared for effectively.

Modern agriculture emerged at the end of the 19th century, with a better knowledge of plant and animal physiology, the availability of energy, and the introduction of machinery for farming and crop processing. The considerable technical progress of the 20th century laid the foundation for the industrialization of agriculture. Advances in chemistry resulted in fertilizers that could make up for deficiencies in poor soil, as well as pesticides and weed killers that protected crops. Although many of these chemicals have proven to be harmful to the environment, they did help bring about amazing leaps in production. Selective breeding has resulted in plant varieties and animal breeds with the most desirable traits.

Current agricultural practices include propagation techniques (using one plant to produce more plants) and hydroponics (growing plants in water, sand, or gravel). The latest advances in agricultural science are in biotechnology, particularly genetic engineering.

Through the years, advances in food preservation have also been made. Advances include sterilization, refrigeration and freezing, and the use of irradiation.

Time line of main food preservation techniques	
1795-1810	Nicolas Appert develops canning method (thermal sterilization)
1850-1860	First forced drying system First absorption refrigerating equipment
1906	Modern freeze-drying techniques are mastered
1910	Canning and forced drying used on an industrial scale
1916	The first home refrigerators make their appearance in the United States
1928	Freezing techniques are invented
1940	Continuous spray, roller and band dryers
1950	Aseptic conditioning is invented Irradiation
1960	Controlled-atmosphere cool maintenance techniques

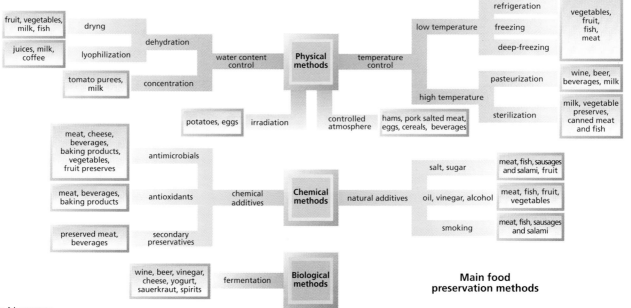

Main food preservation methods

Genetic Engineering

For years, people have been able to influence the characteristics of plants and animals through selective breeding. By breeding plants and animals with certain traits, new generations will eventually possess more desirable characteristics. Selective breeding has resulted in horses that are especially strong or fast, for example, or plants that thrive in particular environments.

Today, however, our ability to change plant and animal species has taken a giant leap forward, due to advances in genetic engineering. This technology involves altering the genetic material, or DNA, of plants and animals. DNA is essentially a blueprint that passes along a set of traits from one generation to the next. By altering DNA, genetic scientists have been able to create plants and animals with specific traits.

In agriculture, genetic engineering has huge potential. It can be used to create plants that are resistant to disease or bear fruit with no seeds, for example, or to create cattle that provide consumers with fatless steaks. Many people are concerned, however, about the possible consequences of genetic engineering. They worry about a loss of variety in natural species and potential risks to both people and the environment.

Genetically modified crops

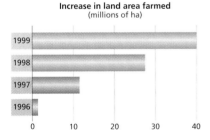

Increase in land area farmed
(millions of ha)

Land area broken
down by country (%)

Argentina 16.8%
Canada 10%
China 0.7%
Other countries 0.6%
USA 71.9%

Pros and Cons of Genetic Engineering

Pros

Yield: Genetically modified crops can increase traditional yields.

Arable land: Crops with higher yields need less cultivated land. Crops can also be genetically modified to survive hostile climate conditions.

Pesticides: The introduction of genetically modified crops that are resistant to insects and disease reduces the need for chemicals.

Soil: Herbicide-resistant crops preserve the soil.

Diet: Genetic engineering can be used to enrich produce lacking vitamins or proteins or remove any unhealthy natural substances (fats) or substances causing allergies (gluten).

Medical applications: Vaccines and drugs can be obtained from genetically modified vegetables.

Costs: Genetically modified crops reduce production costs.

Developing countries: Genetically modified crops can help developing countries combat hunger.

Cons

Loss of biodiversity: A few genetically modified species could eventually replace the world's large variety of natural species.

Gene flow: Genetically modified crops could pass their genes to wild plants, in ways that may be difficult to foresee and control.

Interaction with ecosystems: Modified crops in an ecosystem may alter the soil, other plants, insects, bacteria, and viruses.

Chemicals: Genetically modified seeds often need more fertilizers and insecticides.

Health: Toxic substances or allergens may be found in food obtained from genetically modified animals or crops.

Developing countries: Since most genetic engineering is carried out in wealthy, developed countries, these countries may increase their agricultural dominance over poorer, developing countries.

Food Availability
A Delicate Balance

Today, over 826 million people suffer from chronic undernourishment, and 792 million of them live in developing countries. Over 500 million people are undernourished in Asia and the Pacific regions, with over half living in India. The most dramatic cases of hunger are in Africa. Undernourished people in Africa have an average food deficit (the amount of undernourishment) of over 300 kilocalories per day.

The world food situation is made worse by population growth. Developing countries cannot feed more people, but they have very high rates of population growth. In these countries, increasing the amount of cultivated land to produce more food is almost impossible, due to widespread poverty, a lack of infrastructures (such as roads and canals) and advanced technologies, poor soil, natural disasters and epidemics, wars, and insufficient aid from developed countries.

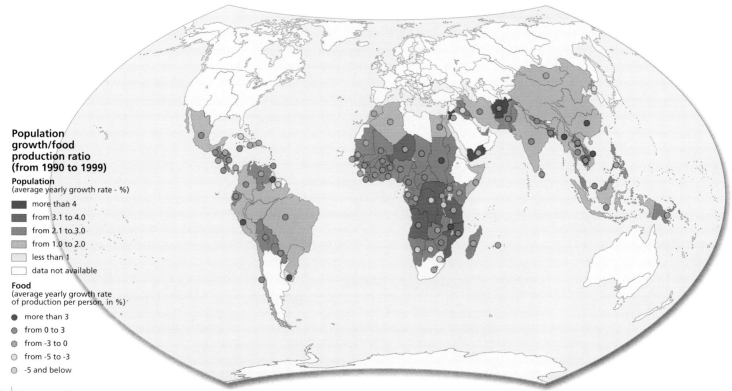

Population growth/food production ratio (from 1990 to 1999)

Population
(average yearly growth rate - %)

- more than 4
- from 3.1 to 4.0
- from 2.1 to 3.0
- from 1.0 to 2.0
- less than 1
- data not available

Food
(average yearly growth rate of production per person, in %)

- more than 3
- from 0 to 3
- from -3 to 0
- from -5 to -3
- -5 and below

World Food Availability

Although undernourishment is still widespread in the world, considerable progress has been made in terms of the quantity and quality of the world's food production. As the United Nations (UN) Secretary General Kofi Annan pointed out at an international meeting about hunger in 2002, our planet is not suffering from a shortage of food. In fact, the world production of cereals alone would be more than enough to meet the minimum nutritional requirements of every person on Earth.

World food availability, however, is extremely uneven. Some countries produce more food than they need. Other countries (particularly ones with high rates of population growth) do not, and they also cannot afford to import the food they need. Today, 20 percent of the world population uses 85 percent of all available food resources. The average expenditure for food consumption in the United States, Canada, northern Europe, and Oceania is estimated to be 60 percent higher than in Africa and 70 percent higher than in Asia.

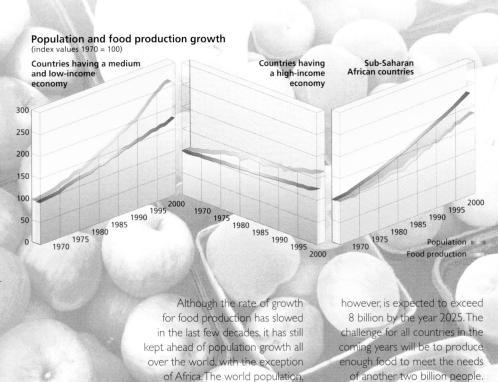

Population and food production growth
(index values 1970 = 100)

Although the rate of growth for food production has slowed in the last few decades, it has still kept ahead of population growth all over the world, with the exception of Africa. The world population, however, is expected to exceed 8 billion by the year 2025. The challenge for all countries in the coming years will be to produce enough food to meet the needs of another two billion people.

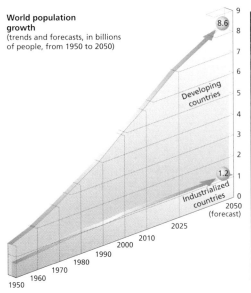

World population growth
(trends and forecasts, in billions of people, from 1950 to 2050)

The most reliable forecasts estimate that future population growth will be driven mainly by countries in Africa, Latin America, and Southeast Asia.

Since 1970, the number of people in the world suffering from undernourishment has declined by 14 percent. Per capita (per person) food availability has increased by 32 percent, but only in wealthier, developed countries.

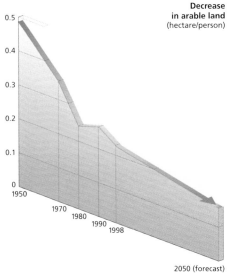

Decrease in arable land
(hectare/person)

To meet the needs of the world's population in the next thirty years, food production has to rise by 75 percent. Per capita availability of arable land, however, is decreasing, due to growing populations and poor soil.

The Magnitude of Hunger

Every day, 24,000 people die because of starvation or diseases related to malnutrition. In the last decade, the number of hungry people has dropped by 2.5 million per year. This figure is far less than the reduction of 24 million people the FAO set as a world objective for 1996, with the ultimate goal of reducing the number of undernourished people to 400 million in the year 2015.

The tragedy of undernourishment mostly takes place in developing countries. In almost all regions of sub-Saharan Africa, for example, more than 35 percent of the population is undernourished. Most of the deaths related to hunger are caused by chronic malnutrition. This malnutrition results in delayed growth, failing sight, a permanent fatigue that makes working impossible, and vulnerability to diseases.

Poverty and disease contribute to the problem of undernourishment. The utter poverty of entire populations prevents them from producing the food they need to survive. The poorest people often live in rural areas. To produce enough food, they would need resources such as quality seeds; effective tools, machinery, and methods; and access to water. In addition, the disease AIDS, which has now spread throughout many African countries,

only worsens the situation by dramatically reducing the number of people available for farming. In addition to increasing production and distribution, some of effects of food shortages could be reduced by providing nutritional information so that people might try to eat more diverse and healthy diets.

Undernourished populations
(variation in number of undernourished, in millions of people, 1990-1999)

Declining

Eastern Asia
Southeast Asia
South America
Western Africa
The Caribbean
North Africa
North America
Central America

Increasing

Southern Africa
Middle East
Eastern Africa
Southern Asia
Central Africa

80 60 40 20 15 10 5 0 5 10 15 20

Undernourished populations
(variation in number of undernourished, 1990-1999)

Declining numbers
more than 1 million
less than 1 million
Unchanged numbers
Increasing numbers
less than 1 million
more than 1 million
data not available

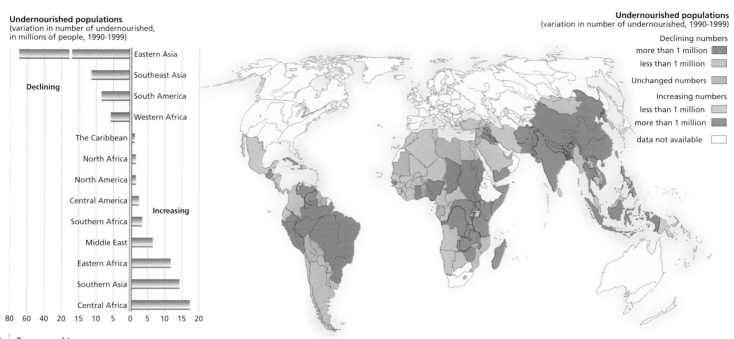

Malnutrition Due to Hunger

All over the world, malnutrition, due to a lack of proteins, calories, vitamins, and vital minerals, causes serious disease and the deaths of millions of people, particularly women and children. Diets that lack iron, iodine, vitamin A, and an appropriate protein and calorie intake seriously weaken a person's immune system, making it vulnerable to diseases and epidemics. The malnutrition of pregnant women often results in the birth of underweight children. If these children survive, they might suffer from delayed growth and retardation, as well as diseases throughout life. Maternal malnutrition can be a vicious cycle: when a pregnant woman has suffered from delayed growth as a girl, she may in turn give birth to an underweight child.

Main diseases related to undernourishment

Anemia

Spread: Affects 2 billion people, mainly women and children. In developing countries, it affects 43% of children up to 4 years, 37% of children between 5 and 12 years, 26% of men and 42% of pregnant women.
Consequences: Impairment of mental development in children; fatigue and limited ability to carry out physical activities, in both children and adults; birth-related mortality; underweight newborns; lower resistance to diseases, and reproductive system disorders.
Prevention: Consumption of at least small amounts of meat, as well as food containing ascorbic acid (vitamin C); avoidance of intestinal parasites, which cause blood loss; enrichment of food with iron (especially children's food).

Protein-Calorie Malnutrition (PCM)

Spread: Causes the deaths of more than 5 million children every year: 80% in Asia, 15% in Africa, and 5% in Latin America.
Consequences: Most lethal form of malnutrition, caused by a diet poor in proteins, carbohydrates, and fats. It causes fatigue, swollen hands and feet, dermatosis, growth stoppage, loss of enthusiasm and interest, and a gradual loss of both fatty tissue and lean body mass. It worsens the consequences of any kind of disease, because it triggers a vicious circle whereby malnutrition alters immune mechanisms and increases susceptibility to infections, which, in turn, worsen the nutritional state.
Prevention: Sufficient nutrition for both the mother and the child; use of energy-providing flour for weaning.

Iodine deficiency

Spread: Affects more than 740 million people in 80 countries.
Consequences: Flaring of the thyroid gland and the formation of a goiter. Most serious consequence is endemic cretinism, a serious mental retardation which is often combined with deaf-mutism, strabismus, and impairments of upright posture and of walking. In its less serious forms, it slows growth, delays mental, motor, and sexual development, and may cause deafness in children; in adults, it causes listlessness, chronic fatigue, limited working capacities, infertility, and early baldness.
Prevention: Consumption of common salt enriched with iodine.

Vitamin A deficiencies (in children up to 6 years of age)

Spread: Vitamin A-related blindness afflicts 2.8 million children under the age of 5; 200 million people in 40 countries suffer from A-avitaminosis.
Consequences: Most serious consequence is xerophtalmia, which initially shows with sight impairment in low light conditions, then degenerates into perforation of the cornea. If it is not treated promptly, xerophtalmia leads to total blindness. Vitamin A deficiency can also reduce resistance to infections and can cause death in children
Prevention: Consumption of oils and fats, food integration with vitamin A (particularly children's food).

2,000   1,600   1,200   800   400   0   40   80   120   160   200
Millions of people affected (estimate)

Undernourishment
(% variation over the total number of undernourished people)

Improving situation

Peru
Chad
Ghana
Kuwait
Mozambique
Malawi
Angola
Sudan
Togo
Thailand
Vietnam
China
Iraq
Guatemala
Mongolia
Somalia   **Worsening situation**
Venezuela
Cuba
Tanzania
Burundi
North Korea
Dem. Rep. of the Congo

-30   -20   -10   0   10   20   30

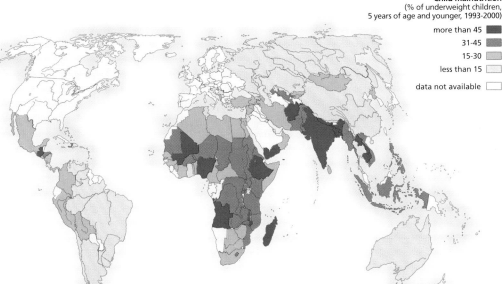

Child malnutrition
(% of underweight children, 5 years of age and younger, 1993-2000)

- more than 45
- 31-45
- 15-30
- less than 15
- data not available

Disasters and Resources

Poverty is not the only cause of hunger and malnutrition in the world. Disasters (natural and man-made) and armed conflicts, with their high toll in human lives and destruction of the environment, also contribute to food shortages.

Although disasters such as hurricanes, floods, and earthquakes can hit rich and poor countries alike, they usually have a much more devastating impact on poor, developing countries. In these countries, people often do not have the means for taking preventative measures against disasters, and they also do not have the resources for surviving a disaster or rebuilding after the disaster has struck. If a disaster results in the loss of crops, livestock, means of production, or infrastructure, poverty will become worse. People will face limited options for work, and development opportunities for the future will be lost.

Today, many countries are at war, and the majority of them are in the poorest regions of the world, such as sub-Saharan Africa. In these countries, the disruption of farming from armed conflict can have terrible consequences, because agriculture is a source of food, foreign currency, and social stability.

Civil war (conflict between opposing groups within a country) can be especially destructive, because civil wars often affect rural areas more than urban centers. These conflicts often involve a struggle over the very resources that are destroyed by war, such as fertile land, water access, crops, and livestock. During a conflict, food production becomes an important asset, and each side attempts to take away the other side's means of production by laying waste to farmland.

To promote agricultural development and reduce hunger in the world, steps will have to be taken to end armed conflicts and provide people with more resources for handling disasters.

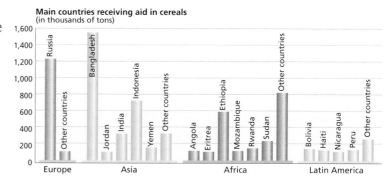

Main countries receiving aid in cereals
(in thousands of tons)

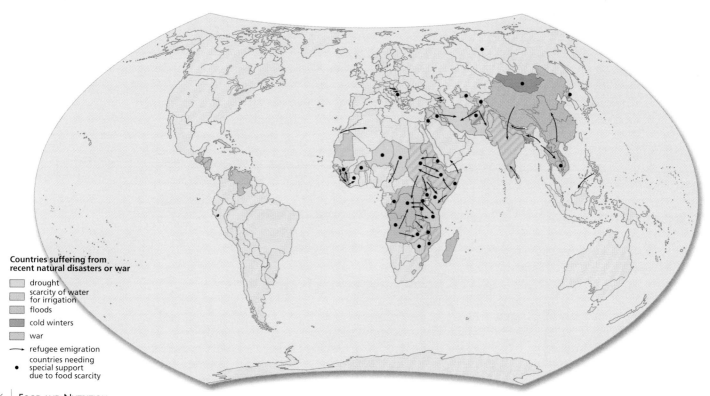

Countries suffering from recent natural disasters or war

- drought
- scarcity of water for irrigation
- floods
- cold winters
- war
- → refugee emigration
- • countries needing special support due to food scarcity

The Many Sides of Natural Disasters

In many developing countries, food production is threatened by drought, floods, hurricanes, tornadoes, extreme temperatures, volcanic eruptions, and earthquakes, as well as by livestock epidemics and insect plagues. Such disasters often force the countries to seek international aid. Some regions of the world, such as tropical areas in Asia and the Americas, are particularly vulnerable to natural disasters, for reasons of geology and climate. In many cases, disasters have terrible consequences for populations that are already struggling with poverty and hunger.

On a global level, natural disasters cause over 150,000 deaths a year and affect 200 million people, most of whom live in poor, developing countries. Natural disasters have occurred in the past and will continue to occur in the future. Climate problems of the last few decades, however, suggest that natural disasters may become more frequent and intense.

Man-made disasters, which include industrial accidents and the effects of pollution and development, can also have an impact on food production. Environmental problems due to human activity include desertification, in which arable land turns to desert; excessively high levels of salt in the soil of arable land; a lack of access to clean water; and the extinction of plant and animal species. Wars also have an impact. They cause masses of people to migrate, traumatize survivors, and leave behind unexploded mines in farming areas.

Refugees (From UNHCR, 2001)

Country of Origin	Main countries offering political asylum	Number
Afghanistan	Pakistan / Iran	3,809,600
Burundi	Tanzania	554,000
Iraq	Iran	530,100
Sudan	Uganda / Ethiopia / Dem. Rep. of the Congo / Kenya / Central African Rep.	489,500
Angola	Zambia / Dem. Rep. of the Congo / Namibia	470,600
Somalia	Kenya / Yemen / Ethiopia / United States / United Kingdom	439,900
Bosnia & Herzegovina	Yugoslavia* / United States / Sweden / Denmark / Netherlands	426,000
Dem. Rep. of the Congo	Tanzania / Congo / Zambia / Rwanda / Burundi	392,100
Vietnam	China / United States	353,200
Eritrea	Sudan	333,100

*from 4-11-2003 Serbia and Montenegro

Once planted, a mine can stay active for over 50 years, hidden underground or in vegetation until someone sets it off. Mining can have a dramatic impact on food production. Farmers are not able to use arable land and pastures that have mines, and mines are often found in infrastructures that are necessary for food production, such as dams, canals, power stations, roads, and railways. Officials estimate that millions of mines are active in 80 countries, causing a victim every 20 minutes. Countries with large amounts of mines include Angola, Afghanistan, Mozambique, and Cambodia.

War and natural disasters often force people to leave their homes and farms and become refugees. The number of refugees is increasing at a frightening pace. Between 1960 and 1975, the number of refugees rose by about 3 million people a year. In 2001, the number of refugees surpassed 20 million, with more than half of the refugees coming from devastated countries in sub-Saharan Africa. In this region of the world, over a dozen countries are facing serious food shortages. To a large degree, these shortages are due to the devastating consequences of conflict between various ethnic groups.

Healthy Eating Habits

While hunger remains widespread in many parts of the world, poor eating habits have also become a problem. In 1995, for example, Americans spent a record $31 billion on pizza—about five times the U.S. government's expenditures for humanitarian aid and support to developing countries. All over the world, obesity is afflicting an increasing number of people. Today, the average daily consumption of calories in industrialized countries is over 3,300, compared to between 2,500 and 2,700 in the 1960s. Obesity has also become a problem in developing countries. Serious health issues related to obesity include heart problems, diabetes, lung and colon cancer, atherosclerosis, and arthrosis.

In the United States, two sets of guidelines for a proper diet have been developed. The first set of guidelines, called Recommended Daily Allowances (RDAs), indicates the amounts of various nutrients that an adult needs in order to avoid becoming sick. The second set of guidelines, known as Optimal Dietary/Daily Allowances (ODAs), indicates the amounts of nutrients an adult needs in order to maintain the best health. These guidelines have proven useful for identifying poor eating habits such as overeating and for helping people establish healthy, balanced diets.

In many countries, health officials create nutrition guidelines, which they tailor to the specific needs and resources of their countries. Through education campaigns, these guidelines can help people focus on the nutritional value of different foods and improve their eating habits.

A lack of physical activity is one factor in causing people to become overweight. Other factors include advertising campaigns and promotions that companies use to get people to buy—and consume—their products. A person might choose a "supersize" serving, for example, when even a "normal" serving is too large from a nutritional standpoint. In addition, many companies sell foods with large amounts of fat, sugar, or salt, which can make food tasty but are not necessarily part of a healthy diet.

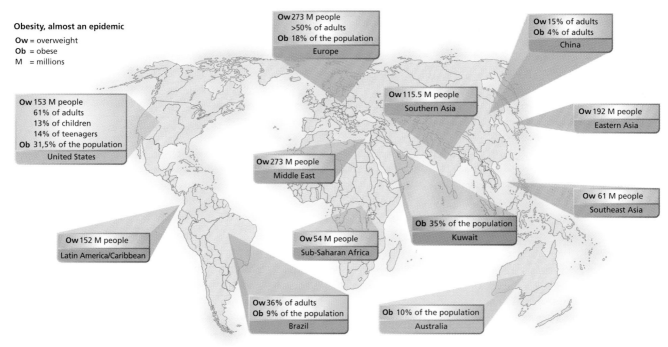

Obesity, almost an epidemic

Ow = overweight
Ob = obese
M = millions

Ow 273 M people
>50% of adults
Ob 18% of the population
Europe

Ow 15% of adults
Ob 4% of adults
China

Ow 153 M people
61% of adults
13% of children
14% of teenagers
Ob 31,5% of the population
United States

Ow 115.5 M people
Southern Asia

Ow 192 M people
Eastern Asia

Ow 273 M people
Middle East

Ow 61 M people
Southeast Asia

Ow 152 M people
Latin America/Caribbean

Ow 54 M people
Sub-Saharan Africa

Ob 35% of the population
Kuwait

Ow 36% of adults
Ob 9% of the population
Brazil

Ob 10% of the population
Australia

Obesity in Developing Countries

The problem of overeating and obesity does not just involve wealthy nations. In Latin America, which has many undeveloped countries, the percentage of underweight children has decreased considerably, but overeating has become more widespread. In Brazil, for example, overeating is now a problem for 36 percent of the population. Obesity is on the rise among the wealthy urban classes of many poor countries where hunger is a problem.

The number of overweight people is growing, particularly in countries experiencing economic improvement. A strong economy can result in better access to different foods, reduced physical activity, and exposure to the diets of wealthier, developed nations. Urbanization can also be responsible for changes in diet. In China and Indonesia, for example, the number of overweight people in the cities is twice what is recorded in rural areas, while in the Congo, obesity is six times more widespread in cities than in rural areas.

People who move from a rural area to a city often abandon their traditional food habits, such as eating a diet high in cereals, fruit, and vegetables and low in sugars and fats. They buy processed food, which is often not very nutritious, and they adopt lifestyles that involve little physical activity, reducing their energy consumption by as much as 50 percent.

Infant obesity deserves special attention, since the number of fatty cells a person has is determined in the first year of life. A child who is overweight at birth will be more likely to gain weight as an adult.

Comparison between undernourished and overfed populations
(in millions of people and % over the overall population)

BMI< 17 (in millions) BMI > = 30 (in millions)
BMI < 17 (in %) *BMI > = 30 (in %)*
BMI = Body Mass Index (millions)

Today, many wealthy, developed countries have more food than their populations need. In most cases, however, this food is not being used to help alleviate hunger in various parts of the world. Instead, the countries are witnessing food waste and overeating, as well as extensive use of substances with high protein value, such as freeze-dried fish or powdered milk, which are mainly used to feed cattle.

The Body Mass Index

The Body Mass Index (BMI) is used to assess an adult's body fat, as well as associated health risks. The index is based on the relationship between a person's weight and height, and it is calculated by dividing weight (in kilograms) by height (in meters) squared. The BMI is considered much more reliable than simple body weight in determining the condition of a person and identifying any potential health risks. Its main shortcoming is that it does not take into account an individual's build, bone structure, and health conditions, and it cannot tell the difference between fatty tissue and muscular tissue. A person who is in good physical good condition, for example, can have the same height and weight, and therefore the same BMI, as someone who does not exercise, But while the two people have the same BMI, they will probably have drastically different physical features. The active person will probably have a lot of lean muscle mass and little fat, while the inactive person will have a lot of fat and not much lean muscle mass.

Body Mass Index (BMI)		
> 40	Grade 3 overweight	Seriusly obese
30 - 40	Grade 2 overweight	Obese
25 - 30	Grade 1 overweight	Overweight
18.5 - 25	Normal weight	Normal
< 18.5	Underweight	Thin

Nutrition and Society
The Role of Women

Women play a vital role in world food production. In most developing countries, women struggle every day against poverty and hunger. Trying to feed their families, they grow crops in very poor soils, using simple tools and no fertilizers. In many Asian and African countries, almost all agricultural production is handled by women, especially when men leave their homes to find jobs in other countries. During periods of drought and famine, women often show considerable ingenuity and adaptability. They may grow alternatives to traditional crops, for example, or find medicinal herbs when no drugs are available, saving entire villages from illness and death.

In these same countries, however, women often have few rights and little power over their lives. They do not own land, have no access to credit, do not share in agricultural profits, and cannot attend technical courses. A woman often has no say in decisions made within her family or in her village, and she cannot take part in political debates. The growing of crops is often considered part of a woman's role as a wife and mother, rather than an important contribution to the national economy. Outside the family, women are paid poorly for agricultural work and are not included in official statistics. If women are going to become more effective in the fight against hunger, they will need equal access to resources and decision-making.

Work Performed by Women in Developing Countries
- Child care
- Cooking of meals
- Collection of firewood
- Water transportation
- Fieldwork
- Cultivation of kitchen gardens
- Storage and preparation of produce
- Sale of surplus produce
- Care of domesticated animals
- Weaving, sewing, and other crafts

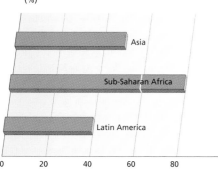

Women's contribution to agricultural production in developing countries
(%)

Asia

Sub-Saharan Africa

Latin America

0   20   40   60   80

In low-income countries where food is scarce, at least 70 percent of working women operate in the agricultural sector and are responsible for food production. Cultivating their own kitchen gardens, they raise crops, such as legumes and other vegetables that contain important nutrients and are often the only foods available.

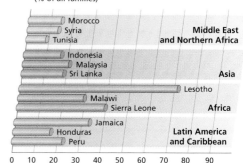

Families managed by women in some developing countries
(% of all families)

Morocco
Syria
Tunisia   **Middle East and Northern Africa**

Indonesia
Malaysia
Sri Lanka   **Asia**

Lesotho
Malawi
Sierra Leone   **Africa**

Jamaica
Honduras   **Latin America and Caribbean**
Peru

0   10   20   30   40   50   60   70   80   90

Street Food

The cooking and selling of food on the street is a very widespread custom, particularly in developing countries. In these countries, street food is an important part of local eating habits. Although it is hard to measure the overall sales of the world's street vendors, an estimated 2.5 billion people eat street food.

In Southeast Asia, women and children manage 70 to 90 percent of street food stalls. Even when street food is sold by men, the work of producing it is usually done by women. The raw materials of street food usually come from small, local gardens.

Street food is usually cheap, fast, and tasty. It reflects local traditions and is often very nourishing. A study done in Kolkata (Calcutta), India, found that a 1,000-calorie street meal contains about 1 ounce (30 g) of proteins, .5 ounces (15 g) of fats, and 6 ounces (180 g) of carbohydrates. Such food is certainly a cheap and effective way to have a nutritionally balanced meal.

Women selling street food in some African countries
(% of the total number of street vendors)

Benin (Cotonou)				
Ghana (Accra)				
Lesotho				
Dem. Rep. of the Congo (Kinshasa)				
Togo				

0   20   40   60   80   100

In many developing countries, street vendors lack clean water and effective refrigeration and cooking systems, and they prepare and sell food in unsanitary conditions. To make street food safer, the FAO has launched a campaign to educate street vendors and food inspectors about the proper ways to cook and store food.

In Bangkok, Thailand, 20,000 street food vendors supply the population with 40 percent of its daily calorie intake. In Kolkata (Calcutta), India, sales of street food is estimated to be almost 100 million dollars a year.

Microcredit

Farmers in developing countries often need money to buy seeds, tools, fertilizers, and pesticides. These farmers usually cannot get loans from large banks because they have no collateral to offer and cannot afford the high interest rates and large loan repayments.

Today, however, a system called microcredit helps farmers get the loans they need. The microcredit system involves banks and other institutions providing very small loans to farmers and other business owners. Through microcredit, even the poorest farmers can have access to loans so they can buy materials and equipment.

After microcredit was implemented, women emerged as ideal candidates for loans. They tend to manage the money very carefully, they are usually committed to spending the money entirely on the improvement of their families' living conditions, and they often take the initiative in establishing new enterprises. When a woman in a developing country becomes more financially independent, the health, diet, and education of other family members, particularly children, also improves.

Microcredit first emerged in the 1970s, when Professor Muhammad Yunus established the Grameen Bank in Bangladesh (where *grameen* means "farmer") for providing small loans and support to poor farmers. The Grameen Bank now has more than 2.5 million members, 95 percent of whom are women.

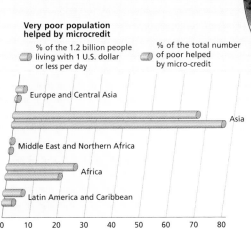

Very poor population helped by microcredit

% of the 1.2 billion people living with 1 U.S. dollar or less per day

% of the total number of poor helped by micro-credit

Europe and Central Asia

Asia

Middle East and Northern Africa

Africa

Latin America and Caribbean

0   10   20   30   40   50   60   70   80

Food as Culture
Languages, Religions, Taboos

Food represents more than just nourishment. Around the world, eating habits reflect specific cultures and environments. Many foods that might be enjoyed in one area of the world are treated with disgust in another region. In the United States, for example, people do not generally eat insects such as locusts, bees, butterfly larvae, or termites. But in some Asian, African, and South American countries, these insects are prized for their high protein content. People in Europe and North America keep dogs and cats as beloved pets, but Korean and Chinese people often cook and eat these animals. Likewise, rabbit meat is a traditional food in France and Italy, but it is less generally eaten in the United Kingdom or North America.

The cultures of different peoples often determine what foods can and cannot be eaten, regardless of their nutritional value. Environmental conditions, economics, and various traditions and customs all help to create a "language" of eating habits that can express certain meanings for a specific culture. In the same way that humans around the world speak different languages, they also have different kinds of foods and food customs.

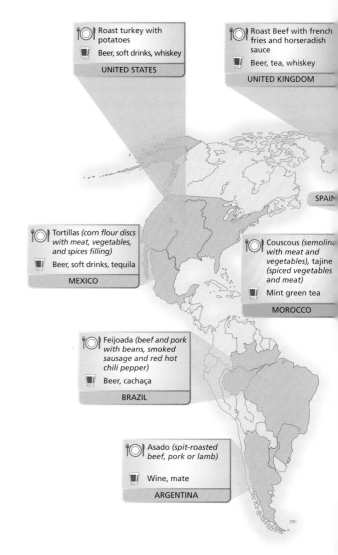

Roast turkey with potatoes
Beer, soft drinks, whiskey
UNITED STATES

Roast Beef with french fries and horseradish sauce
Beer, tea, whiskey
UNITED KINGDOM

SPAIN

Tortillas (corn flour discs with meat, vegetables, and spices filling)
Beer, soft drinks, tequila
MEXICO

Couscous (semolina with meat and vegetables), tajine (spiced vegetables and meat)
Mint green tea
MOROCCO

Feijoada (beef and pork with beans, smoked sausage and red hot chili pepper)
Beer, cachaça
BRAZIL

Asado (spit-roasted beef, pork or lamb)
Wine, mate
ARGENTINA

Like languages, food customs are governed by certain rules. Breaking these rules—by eating the wrong kind of food, for example, or using the wrong cooking methods—can be just as disturbing as a grammatical error in writing or speech.

The "grammar" of meals
Just like the words of a language, foods are organized in ways that are determined by cultural traditions.

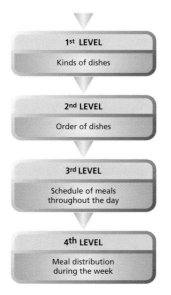

1st LEVEL
Kinds of dishes

2nd LEVEL
Order of dishes

3rd LEVEL
Schedule of meals throughout the day

4th LEVEL
Meal distribution during the week

Meals in different countries are characterized by the dishes themselves (with many dishes being part of a country's specific traditions), the order in which the dishes are served (in the United States and other Western countries, for example, the order is usually appetizer, main course, dessert), and the way in which meals are organized during the day (breakfast, lunch, dinner) and during the week (serving fish only on Friday, for example, or eating a larger meal on Sunday).

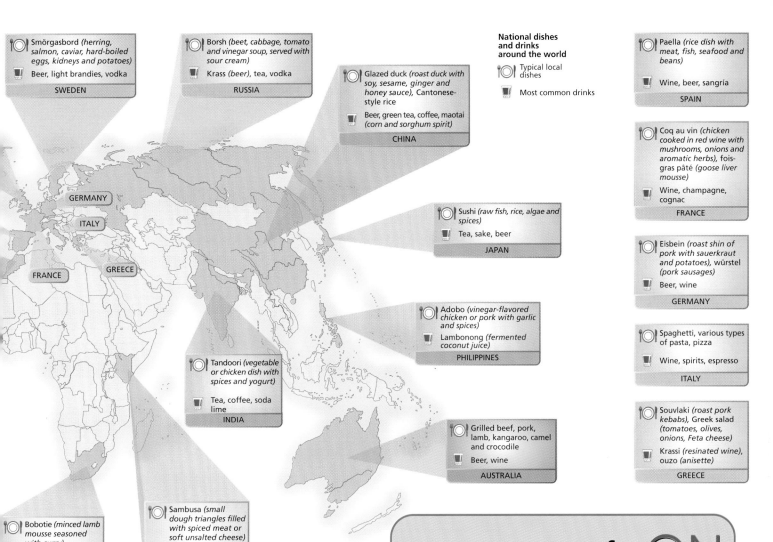

National dishes and drinks around the world

🍽️ Typical local dishes

🥤 Most common drinks

🍽️ Smörgåsbord (herring, salmon, caviar, hard-boiled eggs, kidneys and potatoes)
🥤 Beer, light brandies, vodka
SWEDEN

🍽️ Borsh (beet, cabbage, tomato and vinegar soup, served with sour cream)
🥤 Krass (beer), tea, vodka
RUSSIA

🍽️ Glazed duck (roast duck with soy, sesame, ginger and honey sauce), Cantonese-style rice
🥤 Beer, green tea, coffee, maotai (corn and sorghum spirit)
CHINA

🍽️ Paella (rice dish with meat, fish, seafood and beans)
🥤 Wine, beer, sangría
SPAIN

🍽️ Coq au vin (chicken cooked in red wine with mushrooms, onions and aromatic herbs), fois-gras pâté (goose liver mousse)
🥤 Wine, champagne, cognac
FRANCE

🍽️ Sushi (raw fish, rice, algae and spices)
🥤 Tea, sake, beer
JAPAN

🍽️ Eisbein (roast shin of pork with sauerkraut and potatoes), würstel (pork sausages)
🥤 Beer, wine
GERMANY

🍽️ Adobo (vinegar-flavored chicken or pork with garlic and spices)
🥤 Lambonong (fermented coconut juice)
PHILIPPINES

🍽️ Spaghetti, various types of pasta, pizza
🥤 Wine, spirits, espresso
ITALY

🍽️ Tandoori (vegetable or chicken dish with spices and yogurt)
🥤 Tea, coffee, soda lime
INDIA

🍽️ Grilled beef, pork, lamb, kangaroo, camel and crocodile
🥤 Beer, wine
AUSTRALIA

🍽️ Souvlaki (roast pork kebabs), Greek salad (tomatoes, olives, onions, Feta cheese)
🥤 Krassi (resinated wine), ouzo (anisette)
GREECE

🍽️ Bobotie (minced lamb mousse seasoned with curry)
🥤 Beer, wine
SOUTH AFRICA

🍽️ Sambusa (small dough triangles filled with spiced meat or soft unsalted cheese)
🥤 Beer, cocunut milk, tamarind juice
KENYA

GERMANY, ITALY, FRANCE, GREECE

Food preferences around the world

Animal	Edible/generally eaten	Not generally eaten
Insects	Latin America, Asia, Africa	Western Europe, North America
Dog	Korea, China, Oceania	Europe, North America
Horse	France, Belgium, Italy, Japan	Great Britain, North America
Rabbit	France, Italy	Great Britain, North America
Snail	France, Italy	Great Britain, North America
Frog	France, Italy, Asia	Rest of Europe, North America

In terms of food production, pigs are very profitable animals. They transform 35 percent of what they eat into meat, compared to 12.5 percent for cattle. Piglets grow by 1 pound (.5 kg) for every 4 pounds (2 kg) of food that they eat, compared to 11 pounds (5 kg) for a calf. A sow has a fairly short pregnancy, and litters can include 8 or more piglets. Each piglet will weigh over 400 pounds (180 kg) within 6 months.

focusON

Religions and Food Taboos

Religious practices often shape food habits. Muslims, for example, are not supposed to eat pork, which is considered impure, and they are also not supposed to drink alcohol. Jews are not supposed to eat either pork or shellfish, and they are also not supposed to mix meat and milk or cook on Saturday. Reflecting the sacred status of cows in Hinduism, the main religion of India, the constitution of the country specifically forbids the slaughtering of these animals.

The religious taboo against pork may have actually begun as a practical solution to some specific problems. Long ago, as regions in what is now the Middle East gradually turned to desert, pigs may have become less desirable. They do not have sweat glands and like to plunge into water to cool off, which would have spoiled an already scarce resource. In addition, crops grown for human consumption, such as corn, potatoes, soybeans, and wheat, had to be fed to pigs, who do not eat grass as cows and sheep do. Pigs cannot provide milk or help in the fields. They can also carry the disease trichinosis. The taboo against pork, laid down in the Bible, also existed among various peoples in the region, such as the Phoenicians, the Egyptians, and the Babylonians.

COUNTRIES	Calorie availability (1)	Protein/fat availability (2)	Food imports/ consumption (3)	Undernourished/ rachitic children (4)	Drinking water draw (5)
Afghanistan	1774	-	-	-	1830
Albania	2961	99/79	27/-	-	94
Algeria	2853	79/70	32/-	13/18	160
Andorra	3463	-	-	-	-
Angola	1903	40/37	-	42/53	57
Antigua and Barbuda	2365	81/93	-/33	-	-
Argentina	3093	95/110	5/-	-	1043
Armenia	2371	65/54	31/-	3/8	1145
Australia	3224	107/132	5/14	-	934
Austria	3536	103/161	6/13	-	304
Azerbaijan	2236	66/38	-	10/22	2248
Bahamas	2443	78/81	16/-	-	-
Bahrain	-	-	12/-	9/10	-
Bangladesh	2085	45/22	15/41	56/55	220
Barbados	3176	92/109	17/-	5/7	-
Belarus	3225	94/96	11/16	-	294
Belgium	3619	102/160	10/15	-	917
Belize	2907	65/76	20/28	6/-	109
Benin	2487	59/44	-/45	29/25	26
Bhutan	-	-	21/-	38/56	-
Bolivia	2174	57/57	8/-	10/26	201
Bosnia and Herzegovina	-	-	-	-	-
Botswana	2183	70/60	-/25	17/29	99
Brazil	2974	76/84	10/-	6/11	245
Brunei	2857	83/83	14/-	-	-
Bulgaria	2686	80/90	9/15	-	1544
Burkina Faso	2121	62/47	-	36/31	18
Burundi	1685	51/11	-	37/43	20
Cambodia	2048	47/33	-	52/56	64
Cameroon	2111	48/44	14/38	22/29	37
Canada	3119	98/126	6/9	-	1602
Cape Verde	3015	70/80	-	14/16	-
Central African Rep.	2016	44/64	12/-	27/34	-

COUNTRIES	Calorie availability (1)	Protein/fat availability (2)	Food imports/ consumption (3)	Undernourished/ rachitic children (4)	Drinking water draw (5)
Chad	2032	59/60	24/-	39/40	-
Chile	2796	77/82	7/-	1/2	1626
China	2897	78/71	5/-	10/17	461
Colombia	2597	63/65	12/-	8/15	174
Comoros	1858	43/42	-	26/34	-
Congo	2143	43/50	21/36	17/21	-
Congo, Dem. Rep. of the	1755	28/28	-	34/45	10
Costa Rica	2649	68/80	8/-	5/6	780
Croatia	2445	63/69	10/17	1/1	-
Cuba	2480	52/49	-	-	-
Cyprus	3429	109/147	20/-	-	-
Czech Republic	3244	96/111	6/15	1/2	266
Denmark	3407	108/132	12/10	-	233
Djibouti	2084	44/61	-	18/26	-
Dominica	3059	86/78	26/32	6/11	-
Dominican, Republic	2288	50/74	-	6	445
East Timor	-	-	-	-	-
Ecuador	2679	59/98	12/-	17/34	582
Egypt	3287	89/58	21/44	12/25	956
El Salvador	2562	64/55	16/-	12/23	245
Equatorial Guinea	2230	-	-	-	15
Eritrea	1622	51/20	-	44/38	-
Estonia	2849	95/91	16/-	-	2097
Ethiopia	1858	54/23	14/-	47/51	51
Fiji	2865	74/106	16/30	8/3	-
Finland	3100	101/127	7/11	-	440
France	3518	113/164	10/12	-	665
Gabon	2556	73/55	19/37	-	57
Gambia	2350	50/62	-	26/31	29
Georgia	2614	69/39	-	-	-
Germany	3382	96/144	9/11	-	582
Ghana	2611	49/32	-	25/26	35
Greece	3649	115/153	14/28	-	523

COUNTRIES	Calorie availability (1)	Protein/fat availability (2)	Food imports/ consumption (3)	Undernourished/ rachitic children (4)	Drinking water draw (5)
Grenada	2768	67/93	23/26	-	-
Guatemala	2339	61/46	12/-	24/46	140
Guinea	2231	48/50	-/32	-/29	140
Guinea – Bissau	2430	49/61	-	23/-	11
Guyana	2530	69/54	7/-	12/10	1812
Haiti	1869	41/40	-	28/32	7
Honduras	2403	58/62	16/-	25/39	294
Hungary	3313	85/137	4/14	2/3	660
Iceland	3117	113/121	10/13	-	610
India	2496	59/45	6/-	53/52	612
Indonesia	2886	67/57	11/45	34/42	95
Iran	2836	75/63	-/23	11/15	1362
Iraq	2619	56/77	-	-	4575
Ireland	3565	111/133	7/14	-	233
Israel	3278	105/113	7/-	-	408
Italy	3507	109/147	11/14	-	986
Ivory Coast (Côte d'Ivoire)	2610	50/55	17/35	24/24	67
Jamaica	2553	63/77	17/26	5/6	159
Japan	2932	96/83	16/11	-	735
Jordan	3014	75/86	-	5/8	173
Kazakhstan	3085	97/66	11/-	8/16	2294
Kenya	1976	52/47	14/38	22/33	51
Kiribati	2772	-	-	-	-
Kuwait	3096	97/95	16/-	6/12	525
Kyrgyzstan	2447	82/47	21/-	11/25	2729
Laos	2108	52/26	-	40/47	260
Latvia	2864	79/87	13/-	-	262
Lebanon	3277	85/108	-	3/12	271
Lesotho	2243	64/33	-	16/44	31
Liberia	2044	-	-	-	56
Libya	3289	78/106	23/-	5/15	880
Liechtenstein	3440	-	-	-	-
Lithuania	3261	98/83	11/-	-	1190

COUNTRIES	Calorie availability (1)	Protein/fat availability (2)	Food imports/ consumption (3)	Undernourished/ rachitic children (4)	Drinking water draw (5)
Luxembourg	3530	-	-/10	-	140
Macedonia	2664	69/75	16/-	-	-
Madagascar	2021	46/32	15/-	40/48	1584
Malawi	2043	54/30	-/45	30/48	20
Malaysia	2977	75/87	6/-	18/-	769
Maldives	2485	88/47	-	43/27	-
Mali	2029	61/42	-/48	40/30	162
Malta	3398	110/107	11/-	-	-
Marshall Islands	-	-	-	-	-
Mauritania	2622	74/64	-	23/44	495
Mauritius	2917	72/87	16/24	16/10	410
Mexico	3097	83/88	6/-	8/18	899
Micronesia	-	-	-	-	-
Moldova	2567	69/48	8/28	-	853
Monaco	-	-	-	-	-
Mongolia	1917	71/72	14/-	10/22	273
Morocco	3078	82/61	17/45	9/23	427
Mozambique	1832	35/32	22/-	26/36	55
Myanmar	2862	72/47	-	39/-	101
Namibia	2183	60/38	-	26/28	110
Nauru	-	-	-	-	-
Nepal	2366	61/32	12/37	47/54	150
Netherlands	3284	106/141	11/11	-	518
New Zealand	3395	108/137	9/12	-	589
Nicaragua	2186	49/47	18/-	12/25	367
Niger	2097	61/39	-	50/41	42
Nigeria	2735	62/71	-/48	31/34	41
North Korea	2282	-	-	-	687
Norway	3357	104/136	7/13	-	488
Oman	-	-	17/-	23/23	564
Pakistan	2476	61/65	21/40	26/23	2053
Palau	-	-	-	-	-
Panama	2430	65/68	12/-	7/14	755

COUNTRIES	Calorie availability (1)	Protein/fat availability (2)	Food imports/ consumption (3)	Undernourished/ rachitic children (4)	Drinking water draw (5)
Papua New Guinea	2224	48/42	-	30/43	28
Paraguay	2566	77/79	20/-	5/11	109
Peru	2302	60/50	16/-	8/26	300
Philippines	2366	56/47	9/33	28/30	685
Poland	3366	99/112	8/20	-	321
Portugal	3667	113/132	13/20	-	739
Qatar	-	-	15/-	6/8	-
Romania	3253	100/82	8/24	6/8	1135
Russia	2904	90/81	17/18	3/13	790
Rwanda	2056	46/22	-	27/42	24
St. Kitts and Nevis	2771	75/95	19/30	-	-
St. Lucia	2734	80/72	26/39	-	-
St. Vincent and Grenadine	2472	65/69	25/24	-	-
Samoa	2828	-	-	-	-
San Marino	3458	-	-	-	-
São Tome and Príncipe	2138	44/76	-	-	-
Saudi Arabia	2783	78/79	18/-	14/20	497
Senegal	2418	61/86	-/52	22/23	201
Serbia and Montenegro	3134	-	-	-	-
Seychelles	2487	79/72	20/-	-	-
Sierra Leone	2035	44/58	-/48	29/35	99
Singapore	3121	-	4/14	-	84
Slovakia	2984	81/105	6/17	-	-
Slovenia	3101	103/102	7/13	-	-
Solomon Islands	2122	51/41	16/-	-	-
Somalia	1531	-	-	-	98
South Africa	2990	77/77	5/-	9/23	395
South Korea	3155	86/80	6/21	-	632
Spain	3310	107/145	12/17	-	781
Sri Lanka	2302	52/46	-/38	34/18	503
Sudan	2395	75/75	-	34/33	-
Suriname	2665	65/55	15/-	-	-
Swaziland	2483	60/42	-/27	10/30	-

COUNTRIES	Calorie availability (1)	Protein/fat availability (2)	Food imports/ consumption (3)	Undernourished/ rachitic children (4)	Drinking water draw (5)
Sweden	3194	100/134	7/10	-	341
Switzerland	3223	88/144	6/12	-	173
Syria	3351	86/95	21/-	13/21	435
Taiwan	3101	-	-	-	-
Tajikistan	2001	53/34	-	-	-
Tanzania	1995	49/31	17/-	27/42	35
Thailand	2360	54/47	5/23	19/16	602
Togo	2469	59/50	-	25/22	28
Tonga	2946	-	-	-	-
Trinidad and Tobago	2661	59/71	11/20	7/5	148
Tunisia	3283	88/93	10/35	4/8	317
Turkey	3525	98/101	5/23	8/16	585
Turkmenistan	2306	65/64	9/-	-	-
Tuvalu	-	-	-	-	-
Uganda	2085	45/28	-	26/38	21
Ukraine	2795	78/72	-/21	-	673
United Arabian Emirates	3390	104/109	10/-	14/17	884
United Kingdom	3276	95/141	9/11	-	205
United States	3699	112/143	5/8	1/2	18/70
Uruguay	2816	84/104	11/-	5/8	241
Uzbekistan	2433	70/70	-	19/31	4121
Vanuatu	2700	60/93	20/-	-	-
Vatican City	-	-	-	-	-
Venezuela	2321	59/66	12/-	5/13	382
Vietnam	2484	57/36	-/40	39/34	415
Yemen	2051	54/36	29/-	46/52	328
Zambia	1970	52/30	10/47	24/42	86
Zimbabwe	2145	52/53	7/28	15/32	136
WORLD	2791	74/72	8,5/..	24/28	..

(1) **Calorie availability:** Number of calories available per person daily

(2) **Protein/fat availability:** Average quantity of proteins and fats, in grams, available per person daily

(3) **Food imports/consumption:** Percentage of food imported and consumed every year on overall imports and consumptions

(4) **Undernourished/rachitic children:** Percentage of children aged five and under whose weight is lower than the parameters specified for this age bracket or who suffer from vitamin D deficiency

(5) **Drinking water draw:** Average amount of drinking water, in liters, available per person yearly

- data not available   .. data not quantifiable

Glossary

A

Agriculture
The field of activity that involves the growing of crops, the care and breeding of livestock, and the preparation, processing, and distribution of products derived from crops and livestock.

AIDS
The acronym for acquired immunodeficiency syndrome, a disease affecting the immune system that is caused by an infectious virus known as HIV. People suffering from AIDS can be vulnerable to a variety of life-threatening diseases.

Allergen
A substance, such as pollen, that can cause a person to have an allergic reaction.

Amino acids
Substances that are the building blocks of proteins. When the body digests food, it breaks down proteins into amino acids. These amino acids play several important roles in the body. They are necessary for the growth of cells, for example, and for the creation of hormones and enzymes.

Anemia
A blood condition involving a decrease of red blood cells, which carry oxygen to different parts of the body. Anemia can be caused by a poor diet, such as a diet lacking in iron.

Animal husbandry
A field of agriculture that involves the care and breeding of domestic animals, or livestock, including cattle, pigs, sheep, and poultry.

Antimicrobials
Substances that can kill or slow the growth of microscopic organisms.

Antioxidants
Substances that prevent oxygen from breaking down food or tissues in the body.

Aquaculture
The care and breeding of fish in a controlled area, as opposed to catching fish in the open sea.

Arable
Suitable for growing crops.

Arthrosis
A disease, affecting the body's joints, that becomes progressively worse over time.

Ascorbic acid
A vitamin substance, commonly called vitamin C, that helps bones, teeth, and blood vessels stay healthy; helps prevent the body's tissues from breaking down; helps the body absorb iron; and plays an important role in the healing of wounds and burns.

Atherosclerosis
A medical condition that involves a buildup of substances, such as cholesterol, on the inner walls of blood vessels. This condition results in a decrease of blood flow and can lead to heart attacks or strokes.

B

Bacteria
A large group of single-celled, microscopic organisms. Bacteria are crucial to life cycles on Earth, because they turn dead organisms and organic waste into substances that can be used by plants. They play a role in certain processes in the human body and are used to create certain food products, such as cheese, yogurt, and beer. Bacteria also cause food to spoil, can lead to food poisoning, and are responsible for many diseases.

C

Calcium
A mineral found in Earth's crust and which is also present in plants and animals. In humans, calcium is the main substance in teeth and bones. Dairy products and certain plant crops are sources of calcium.

Calorie
A unit of measurement for the amount of energy a food provides to the human body when consumed. In science, a small, or gram, calorie equals the heat required to raise one gram of water from 14.5°C to 15.5°C. In dietary terms, a calorie actually refers to a large calorie, or kilocalorie, which equals 1,000 small calories.

Carbohydrates
Organic (derived from plants or animals) substances usually made up of carbon, hydrogen, and oxygen. Green plants create carbohydrates from carbon dioxide and water through photosynthesis. An important source of energy for the human body, carbohydrates can be found in cereals, fruits, and legumes. Sugars such as glucose are simple carbohydrates. Complex carbohydrates, such as starch, consist of several sugars joined together.

Cereals
A group of grasses that are cultivated for their seeds (grain). Cereal crops include wheat, rice, corn, barley, rye, oat, millet, and sorghum. Grown since ancient times, they are rich in starches and proteins.

Cholera
An infectious disease, caused by bacteria found in food and water, that causes diarrhea. Other symptoms include vomiting, excessive thirst, and muscle cramps. If not treated, cholera can lead quickly to death. Clean water and food can prevent outbreaks of cholera.

Climate
A set of weather conditions (temperature, wind, and precipitation) for a particular region of Earth.

Collateral
Something of value, such as property, that a person seeking a loan agrees to give to the lender if the loan is not paid back. Most lenders require some kind of collateral before giving out a loan.

Consultive Group on International Agricultural Research (CGIAR)
An association of various private and public organizations. CGIAR supports a network of agricultural research centers that seek to improve agricultural practices in developing countries.

Cooperative
In agriculture, an organization of farmers that usually helps its members find lower prices for farming supplies and equipment and higher prices for crops. Cooperatives may also provide loans.

Cultivate
To prepare soil so it can be used for raising crops, or to engage in any activity that contributes to the growth of crops.

Crustaceans
Organisms, usually found in the sea, that have external skeletons and antennae, among other features. Crustaceans include lobsters, shrimp, and crabs.

D

Debt
Something, such as money, that a borrower owes to a lender, such as a bank.

Desalination

A process that removes salt from a substance. In various regions of the world, desalination plants are used to create freshwater by removing salt from seawater.

Developed country

A country that is industrialized, with a high level of manufacturing and technology, highly developed infrastructure, and a relatively high standard of living for a large segment of its population.

Developing country

A country that is in the process of becoming industrialized and has a relatively low standard of living for a large segment of its population.

Diabetes

A disease that involves high levels of sugar in the blood stream and is caused by problems with insulin, the hormone that regulates sugar in the body. One kind of diabetes is typically found in people who are overweight. If untreated, diabetes can cause damage to various parts of the body and can lead to death.

Diet

The food and drink that a person consumes on a regular basis. Diets can vary, in both quantity and quality, among different people and in different regions of the world. They are based on factors such as wealth, culture, and food availability.

Distillation

A process that involves boiling a liquid to separate its components. Some alcoholic beverages are created by distilling a fermented substance. When the substance is boiled, alcohol turns into a vapor (gas) before the other components, thereby separating from them, and then returns to liquid form through cooling. Distilled alcoholic beverages include whiskey (made from fermented cereal grains) and rum (made from fermented molasses).

DNA

The abbreviation for deoxyribonucleic acid, which is the chemical in the cells of organisms that contains genetic instructions. DNA is the blueprint for living things, determining the characteristics of organisms.

Drought

A period of extremely dry weather.

E

Embargo

A ban on commercial activity between one country and another. Countries often use embargos as a way to influence the policies or actions of other countries. An embargo can be total or involve certain products. The U.S. embargo against Cuba has been in effect since the 1960s.

Enzyme

A substance that helps speed up the synthesis (joining together) or breakdown of substances.

European Food Information Council (EUFIC)

Independent, non-profit organization established in 1993 to provide European consumers with information on nutrition and food safety.

F

Fatigue

Extreme tiredness; exhaustion.

Fats

Organic compounds, found in both plants and animals, that can provide the human body with very concentrated sources of energy. A compact fuel, fat is stored by the body for later use. In many developed countries where people eat fat-rich diets and are not physically active, accumulation of body fat has become a health issue. Eating too many foods high in fats may lead to heart disease and other health problems.

Fermentation

The breakdown of organic substances brought about by enzymes. In the making of fermented alcoholic beverages, microscopic organisms create enzymes that break
down the sugars in various foods—such as cereals (beer) and grapes (wine)—to produce alcohol.

Fertilizer

A substance, natural or man-made, that adds nutrients to the soil to help plants grow. When arable land is first planted with crops, it usually contains all the nutrients necessary for plant growth. If crops are grown in a particular area for many years, however, nutrients in the soil become depleted, and fertilizers have to be added.

Fiber

Substance in food that cannot be digested. Also called roughage, it helps in moving waste through the intestines and provides several health benefits. Foods containing fiber include green, leafy vegetables and fruit.

Food and Agriculture Organization (FAO)

An agency of the United Nations (UN) that was established in 1945 to improve agricultural production, nutrition, and standards of living around the world, particularly in rural areas. It is based in Rome, Italy.

G

Gene bank

A place that preserves genetic (DNA) samples of various plant or animal species, as well as information relating to those samples. Samples of plant genes might take the form of seeds, pollen, or whole plants. In addition to preserving a diverse collection of species, plant gene banks provide many species with which to create new varieties through genetic engineering.

Genetic engineering

A method of changing plant and animal species by altering their genes, which are the parts of DNA that determine an organism's characteristics. Genetic engineering can be used to create new plant varieties with certain desirable characteristics, such as resistance to disease or higher yields. Plants created through genetic engineering are called genetically modified (GM) crops.

Glaciers

Huge masses of ice that move slowly across land.

Glucose

A kind of carbohydrate found in many plants. Known as a simple sugar, it is the carbohydrate most widely used in body tissues to produce energy. The human body breaks down substances (such as milk and starch found in plants) to use the glucose contained in them.

Gluten

Protein mixture found in cereal grains. Gluten gives bread dough its spongy texture and causes it to rise.

Guinea worm

A parasite (lives within the human body) that enters the body through the drinking of unclean water.

H

Himalayas

A mountain range located in South Asia.

Hormones

Substances in the human body that regulate various processes, such as organ functions and growth.

Hunter-gatherer

A term describing people who get their food by hunting, fishing, and gathering, rather than by planting crops and raising livestock. Before the rise of agriculture, all humans were hunter-gatherers.

Hybrid

The offspring of two different species or varieties.

Hydroponics

An agricultural method that involves growing plants in a material other than soil, such as sand, gravel, or a water solution, which is treated with the necessary plant nutrients found in soil.

I

Industrial revolution

The shift from an agriculture-based economy to one based on large-scale, mechanized manufacturing of goods. The industrial revolution began in Great Britain in the late 18th century. It spread to the United States and Europe in the 19th century and other parts of the world in the 20th century.

Infrastructure

All the structures and systems that a region or country needs to function properly, such as roads, highways, bridges, canals, dams, and services for electricity, communications, and transportation.

Interest

An amount of money that a lender, such as a bank, charges to a borrower. The interest is usually a percentage of the amount that has been borrowed.

International Union of Nutritional Sciences (IUNS)

Organization established in London, England, in 1948 that seeks to make advances in nutritional science through cooperation between nutrition scientists.

International Whaling Commission (IWC)

An organization established in 1946 to protect whale populations and regulate the whaling industry. Today, it includes representatives from many countries around the world. The commission's measures have included banning the whaling of certain species, setting limits on the size and number of whales caught, and making certain regions of the world's oceans off-limits to whaling.

Iodine

A mineral that the human body needs in order to create certain hormones.

Iron

A mineral that is vital for the human body, since it helps form hemoglobin, a substance in red blood cells that carries oxygen through the body. A lack of iron in a person's diet can lead to anemia.

Irradiation

A method of preserving food that involves exposing food to radiation in order to kill bacteria, insects, and other organisms. Radiation is a form of energy that, in high enough doses, can be lethal to organisms (including people). It is also used for making X-rays and for treating certain cancers.

Irrigation

The use of an artificial (other than rainfall) method of watering land so that plants will grow. Irrigation is used for farming in areas that do not get enough rainfall.

L

Lactose

A sugar found in milk. An enzyme in the body called lactase breaks down lactose into the simple sugars galactose and glucose. People who do not have a lot of lactase may have trouble digesting dairy products.

Land reclamation
The process of creating more arable land.

Latitude
A distance, measured in degrees, going north or south from the equator (an imaginary line circling Earth, dividing it into the Northern and Southern Hemispheres.)

Legumes
The common name for leguminous plants, as well as for the fruits they bear. Legumes include peas, beans, peanuts, and soybeans.

Livestock
Domesticated animals used in agriculture. Livestock include cattle, sheep, goats, chickens, and pigs.

Lyophilization
A method for preserving food that is commonly called freeze-drying. The method generally involves freezing a food and then removing the water in it through a special process.

Magnesium
A mineral that is present in most foods. The human body needs magnesium to function properly.

Maté
A tea that is common in South America. It is made from the dried, ground leaves of certain holly plants.

Millet
The common name for a group of cereal grasses. Hardy plants that ripen quickly, millets are cultivated in many poorer agricultural regions of the world. They are a staple food in Asia, Africa, and countries once belonging to the former Soviet Union. In the United States, millet is mostly grown for livestock feed.

Minerals
Inorganic (not derived from plants or animals) substances that the human body needs in order to function properly. Important minerals include calcium, iodine, magnesium, potassium, and sodium.

Mollusks
A group of animals that includes clams, snails, and mussels.

Multinational
Having to do with several countries. A multinational corporation, for example, typically owns companies in many different countries.

Must
The juice of fruit, in particular grapes. Wine is made from fermented grape must.

Pasteurization
A process that heats a liquid, in particular milk, to destroy any bacteria contained in it.

Pesticide
Anything used to kill organisms (such as insects) that are harmful to people or crops. In agriculture, pesticides are often chemicals that are sprayed or dusted on crops.

Photosynthesis
The process by which plants use the energy of sunlight to turn carbon dioxide and water into food. Plants create carbohydrates through the process of photosynthesis.

Physiology
The various processes of a living thing, as well as the branch of science that studies those processes.

Potassium
A mineral that plays many important roles in the functioning of the human body. Citrus fruits and certain vegetables and fish are good sources of potassium.

Proteins
Substances that make up living things. Proteins are necessary for many processes in organisms, including humans. In the human body, for example, proteins are responsible for carrying oxygen through the body, making muscles contract, and clotting blood, and they make up bones, skin, and hair. Proteins in food help build and maintain cells and also provide energy. Although plants can provide proteins, the best protein sources are meat, dairy products, and eggs.

Pulses
A name for the seeds of certain leguminous plants, as well as a name for the plants themselves. Pulses include peas, beans, and lentils.

R

Rachitic
Having to do with rachitis, a disease that is more commonly called rickets. Children who do not have enough vitamin D in their diet may get rickets, which involves the improper development or hardening of bones. Rickets can lead to curving of the spine or legs.

Roselle
A kind of herb used to make tea. Some people drink roselle tea as a treatment for colds and sore throats.

S

Savannah
A tropical grassland. Savannahs can be found in Africa and South America.

Schistosomiasis
A disease caused by worms called flukes (schistosomes) that can live in the human body. When young they live in water, where they can infect humans. Schistosomiasis can lead to death if untreated. Most infected people live in sub-Saharan Africa. Prevention measures include avoiding water infested with flukes.

Sodium
A mineral that has several important uses in the human body, such as regulating fluids and helping muscles to function properly. Sodium can be found in milk, spinach, and other foods, as well as in table salt (sodium chloride).

Sorghum
The common name for a group of cornlike grasses that are native to Africa and Asia. Sorghum grain is a staple food in China, India, and Africa. In the United States, sorghums are primarily grown for livestock feed. Sorghums are extremely hardy plants that can withstand the effects of heat and drought.

Soviet Union
A former communist nation that consisted of Russia and neighboring republics in northwest Asia and Eastern Europe. The Soviet Union was established in 1922, after World War I. It broke apart in 1991.

Staple food
A main food in a particular diet.

Starch
A complex carbohydrate. It is mainly found in grains, legumes, and tubers such as potatoes.

Steppe
Mostly treeless grassland plains found in Eastern Europe and central Asia (Russia). Some portions of the steppe are used for growing crops. This term can also refer to other areas of the world with similar features, such as prairies in the midwestern United States.

Sterilization
In the case of food preservation, any process used to kill organisms, such as bacteria, that are harmful to humans. Pasteurization is a form of sterilization.

Sub-Saharan
Having to do with any region south of the Sahara, a desert region located in northern Africa.

Subsistence farming
A kind of farming that produces most or all of the crops for survival but does not produce any additional crops that can be sold for a profit. Subsistence farming is practiced in many poor rural areas.

Subtropical
Having to do with any region that is close to the tropics (an area, circling Earth at or near the equator, where the Sun is almost directly overhead all year and where temperatures are consistently warm).

T

Temperate
Having to do with the regions of Earth between the tropics and the arctic circle (the most northern area of the Northern Hemisphere) and the antarctic circle (the most southern area of the Southern Hemisphere).

Toxicity
The level of poison in a substance.

Trachoma
A contagious infection of the eye that is caused by bacteria. The infection is spread through physical contact or by flies. It can result in blindness, but in its early stages it responds well to treatment. Trachoma is a major cause of blindness in some villages in northern Africa and often occurs among people living in unclean conditions.

Tributary
A small stream or river that feeds into a larger river

Tropical
Having to do with the tropics (an area, circling Earth at or near the equator, where the Sun is almost directly overhead all year and where temperatures are consistently warm).

Tundra
Arctic plains. Tundra regions have harsh winters and short summers, little rainfall or snowfall, and low-lying plants, such as moss. Tundra can also be found in high mountainous areas and in Antarctica.

U

United Nations (UN)
An international organization established in 1945 to maintain peace and security in the world and promote cooperation among nations.

United Nations High Commissioner for Refugees (UNHCR)
An agency established in 1950 to protect refugees (people who flee their home countries to escape war, natural disaster, or persecution) and solve worldwide refugee problems. The agency is one of the main humanitarian organizations in the world and has won the Nobel Peace Prize twice, in 1954 and 1981.

V

Vitamins
Organic (derived from plants or animals) substances in food that are necessary for the health, growth, and proper functioning of the human body. Important vitamins include vitamin C (ascorbic acid), vitamin A, vitamin D, and vitamin E.

Vitamin A

A vitamin that is necessary for the development and health of skin, bones, and teeth. Lack of vitamin A can lead to difficulty seeing in the dark. Vitamin A can be found in vegetables such as carrots, broccoli, spinach, and squash, as well as in milk, butter, cheese, egg yolks, liver, and fish-liver oils.

Vitamin D

An essential vitamin for the proper development and growth of bones. Vitamin D is also called the sunshine vitamin because it is formed in the body by the action of sunlight on the skin. It is found in egg yolks, liver, tuna, and vitamin D-fortified milk. Children who do not get enough vitamin D in their diet may develop a disease called rachitis, or rickets, which can lead to curving of the spine or legs.

Vitamin E

A vitamin that plays a role in forming red blood cells, muscles, and other tissues. It is found in vegetable oils, margarine, cereals, liver, and green, leafy vegetables. Vitamin E is believed to protect against aging.

W

World Bank

A UN organization, established in 1944, that grants loans to help various countries. The World Bank has provided loans, for example, to increase agricultural production and improve health care, education, and housing in many developing countries. The World Bank's headquarters is located in Washington, D.C.

World Health Organization (WHO)

A specialized UN organization that seeks to improve the health of people around the world, particularly people in poor, developing nations. It was created in 1946 and has its headquarters in Geneva, Switzerland. WHO supplies information on diseases, nutrition, child health, clean living conditions, and other health issues. It promotes international cooperation in medical research and the fight against diseases.

World Trade Organization (WTO)

An international organization, established in 1995, that seeks to increase and improve free trade between nations. The organization now has over 140 member countries. It has a system for settling disputes but has no enforcement powers.

Y

Yield

In agriculture, the amount of food that is produced through cultivation.

Index

Page numbers in *italics* indicate illustrations.

agriculture
   machinery, *38*
   reforms, 35
   rise of, 17, 24, *25*
agro-business see commercial farming
AIDS (acquired immune deficiency syndrome), 54
alcoholic beverages, 32
amino acids, *19*
anemia, 55
animal breeding see livestock
anti-oxidants, 21
aquaculture (fish farming), 37, *37*
ascorbic acid see Vitamin C

bacteria, *23*
barley, 30, *30*, 45
basmati rice, 29, *29*
beer, 32, *32*
beverages, 32–33, 62–63
"biopiracy," 29
Body Mass Index (BMI), 59
bread, 28, *28*

calories, 16, *18*
carbohydrates, 16, 20
carnivores, 18
cereals, 17, 26, 30, *38*, 40, *40*, 42, 44, 45, 47, 53, *56* see
  also specific cereal (e.g., rice)
children
   malnutrition in, 55
   obesity in, *58*, 59
China, 23, 28, *41*, 42, *42*
cholera, *23*
citrus fruits, 21, *39*
Coca-Cola, 33
cocoa, *44*, 49
coffee, *33*, *44*, *47*, 49
commercial farming, 34, *35*, 46–48
computers in agriculture, 38
corn (maize), 30, *30*, *31*, 45
Cuba, 49, *49*

desert reclamation, 38, 39, *39*
diarrhea, *23*

disasters, 56–57, *56*
domesticated animals see livestock
donkeys, 27
drip-irrigation, 39, *39*

European Food Information Council (EUFIC), 17

FAO see Food and Agriculture Organization
fats, 16, 17, 20
fertilizers, *38*, 40, 41, *41*, 50
fiber, 17
fish farming (aquaculture), 37, *37*
fishing, 36, *36*, 37
fish production and consumption, *19*, *43*, 45
Food and Agricultural Organization (FAO) (UN
   agency), *19*, 40, 41, 61
food chain, 18
food preservation, *50*
food production levels, 42
food pyramids, 20, *21*
food taboos, 63, *63*

genetic engineering, *47*, 51
grapes, *32*
"green revolution," *40*, 40–41
Guinea worm, *23*

herbivores, 18
honey, 17
horses, 27
hunger, 52–55
hunter-gatherers, 17, *24*

India, 29, *29*, 41, *41*, 42, *42*
industrialization, 17
insectivores, 18
intestinal worms, *23*
iodine deficiency, 55
irrigation, 38, 39
Israel, 38, 39

lactose intolerance, 25
land mines, *57*
livestock, 26, 26–27, *34–35*, 36, *36*, *47*

maize see corn
malnutrition, 54–55
meals around the world, 62, 62–63
meat, 19, 43, 45, 47
micro-credit, 61, 61
milk, 19, 25
minerals, 16, 20
Missouri River, 38
monoculture, 48, 49
multinational companies, 46–47, 47

National Academy of Sciences, 19
Nestlé, 47, 47

obesity, 58–59, 58, 59
Oldways, 21
omnivores, 18
Optimal Dietary/Daily Allowances (ODAs), 58

Pakistan, 29, 29
peanuts, 30, 31
Pepsi-Cola, 33
pesticides, 38, 40, 41, 47, 50
photosynthesis, 18
pivots (sprinklers), 39, 39
population growth, 52, 53
pork, as banned food, 63, 63
potatoes, 30, 31
poultry farming, 36
protein-calorie malnutrition (PCM), 55
proteins, 16, 17, 20

qariat systems, 39
quinoa, 19, 19

Recommended Daily Allowances (RDAs), 58
refugees, 57
religion, food taboos linked to, 63
rice, 28–29, 29, 40, 41, 42, 45
RiceTec, 29
salt, 17
schistosomiasis, 23
scurvy, 21
soft drinks, 32, 33
sorghum, 30, 30, 31
soybeans, 30, 31, 45

starches, 17
street food, 61, 61
subsistence farming, 34, 35
sugar
    milk (lactose), 25
    as monocultural crop, 49, 49
    refined, 17

tea, 33, 44, 49
trachoma, 23
trade, 44–45, 45
tropical products, 47

United Kingdom, 17
United States Department of Agriculture (USDA), 21

vitamin A deficiencies, 55
vitamin C, 21
vitamins, 16, 20

water, 22–23, 23, 32
whale hunting, 43
wheat, 28, 28, 41, 45
wine, 32, 32
women, 41, 60, 60–61, 61
World Bank, 23

zebras, 27

Photographic references
Archivio IGDA: 16, 17c, 24; C. Baraggi 28; M. Bertinetti 31b, 32-33, 35b; W. Buss 42b; N. Cirani 17a,19, 43; G. Cozzi 49c; A. Dagli Orti 33a; Dani-Jeske 49b; A. De Gregorio 30b; EOSAT 39a; F. Galardi 27b; M. Leigheb 33b; C. Maury 20; NASA 22b; G. Negri 30a; C. Novara 41a; Pubbli Aer Foto 34; C. Sappa 35d, 39b, 40, 42a; G. Sioen 27a, 35c, 37b; A. Tessore 29, 41 b; E. Turri 17b, 23, 35a; S. Vannini 21; A. Vergani 31a, 32a, 37a, 46a, 47.

C. Aid/C. Griffiths/F. Speranza 57a; Anzenberger/R. Froese/F. Speranza 32b; A. Bacchella/F. Speranza 33c; N. Cobbing/F. Speranza 51b; M. Cooper/F. Speranza 60; J.P. Degas/Ask Images/F. Speranza 59a; J. Etchart/F. Speranza 57d; Gable/Jerrican/F. Speranza 59b; R. Giling/ F. Speranza 44, 52, 55; Halsey Creativ Service/Stockfood/F. Speranza 50; R. Holmgren/F. Speranza 51a; Jerrican/V. Deplanne/F. Speranza 58; S. Noorani/F. Speranza 61b; H. Pederesen/F. Speranza 62; K. Prempool/UNEP/F. Speranza 57b; L. Rubin/F. Speranza 39c; H. Schwarzbach/F. Speranza 54; Sdp/F. Renault/F. Speranza 25b; R. Soncin Gerometta/F. Speranza 63; Still Pictures/M. Edwards/F. Speranza 49a; Stockfood/M. Chris/F. Speranza 25a; G. Trotter/F. Speranza 57c.

G. Cappelli/Pandaphoto 53b; S. McKinnon/Pandaphoto 61a

PhotoDisc: 22a, 38, 53a.

Cover: PhotoDisc.